Ridgway Community Church
P.O. Box 322
685 West Sherman Street
Ridgway, CO 81432-0322

A MOMENT'S NOTICE

RECOGNIZING THE SEASON
OF JESUS' APPEARING

A MOMENT'S NOTICE

RECOGNIZING THE SEASON
OF JESUS' APPEARING

by
Hilton Sutton Th.D.

Harrison House
Tulsa, Oklahoma

A Moment's Notice
Recognizing the Season of Jesus' Appearing
ISBN 1-57794-066-0
Copyright © 1998 by Hilton Sutton
Mission to America
736 Wilson Road
Humble, Texas 77338

Published by HARRISON HOUSE, Inc.
P.O. Box 35035
Tulsa, Oklahoma 74153

CONTENTS

PREFACE

Throughout the Church Age, believers have looked and longed for the appearing of Jesus. It is evident from the writings of the apostle Paul that he was surely numbered among those who were aware of the prophetic event.

The glorious appearing of Jesus for the express purpose of receiving a glorious church to Himself, is a very visible event in the prophetic picture of God's Word.

Because of the anxious anticipation of this event, numerous dates have been set by religious groups and individuals. None have been correct, nor will any further date setting be accurate.

However, the apostle Paul is certain when he writes concerning our awareness of the coming of the "Thief in the night." He points out that although we may not know the exact time of the appearing of Jesus and the catching away of the Church, we can know the season in which this prophetic event will occur.

Without question we are now in that season, and are receiving, "a moment's notice."

DEDICATION

I personally give thanks to the Holy Spirit Who has been my teacher. He has guided me through the chapters of this book; to God be the Glory.

I also want to thank those of my staff and members of the editorial department of Harrison House Publishers for their faithful assistance.

I dedicate this book to the Body of Christ, the Church. It is my prayer that all who read these pages will be inspired to serve the Lord diligently and never cease in their effort to win souls.

My sincere gratitude to my loving wife and daughters for their understanding and support.

Hilton Sutton

FOREWORD

In Matthew 16, the Pharisees and Sadducees wanted Jesus to give them a sign as proof of His Messiahship. Knowing the evil intent of their hearts, He rebuked them: "O ye hypocrites, ye can discern the face of the sky; but can ye not discern the signs of the times?"

These religious men could predict the weather. In fact Rabinnical schools taught weather lore. Yet, for all their theology and education, they didn't have eyes to see or minds to discern or recognize eternally important and significant spiritual events. Consequently, they missed the Messiah, the One they were supposedly waiting for. Jesus Christ had no effect in their lives because they couldn't discern the times.

The earth is in the last of the last days. Jesus will return soon. And unless we are discerners of the times and seasons, we won't be ready when He comes.

This is the reason why I am so excited about this book. The Body of Christ needs to know how to recognize the season of the Lord's appearing. We don't want to be led astray. We don't want to become discouraged in waiting. We don't want to miss Jesus' second coming like the Pharisees and Sadducees missed His first.

My friend of 30 years, Hilton Sutton is a precious man of God, a scholar, and a person of prayer. Let his book instruct you and encourage you in *A Moment's Notice: Recognizing the Season of Jesus' Appearing.*

Dr. Doyle "Buddy" Harrison
Founder and Chairman
Harrison House Publishers

CHAPTER 1

THE SEASON OF JESUS' APPEARING

THE SEASON OF JESUS' APPEARING

Through the years I have encountered believers and teachers who have said, "If I could find sufficient evidence to support the Rapture occurring prior to the Tribulation, I would believe it." And every time I have heard a comment like that, I have thought, "What scriptures are you reading?" My friends, God's book is filled with information that focuses on the catching away, or the "Rapture" of the Church. The weight of evidence in Scripture is overwhelming to substantiate its imminent coming. What we don't know is the day or the hour of its coming because Jesus said:

> *But of that day and that hour knoweth no man, no, not the angels which are in heaven, neither the Son, but the Father.* —MARK 13:32

So when someone sets an exact date, forget it. Don't follow that person's predictions. Setting a date for the

glorious appearing of Jesus, designed for the express
purpose of catching away a glorious church, is in rebellion
against the Scripture. No one should follow anyone who is
in rebellion. Multitudes did back in 1988 when a little
book appeared entitled, "88 Reasons Why Jesus Will
Come in 1988." It seemed that Jesus missed that opportunity. So they reset the date for 1989. The teachings of
Jesus were set aside for one's personal belief. Jesus
further states that we are not likely to know the week,
the month nor the year.[1] The *season* of His appearing,
however, *was* made known by Jesus, the apostle Paul,
and the prophets in Scripture. We are now in that season.

In the following pages of this book I will show you,
from the Word of God, that we are in the season of His
appearing. The Lord is soon to appear for the express
purpose of receiving unto Himself a glorious church.

The glorious church that Jesus is returning for will
be made up of people who have purified themselves
because of their hope of His appearing as so instructed in
1 John 3:3:

*And every man that hath this hope in him
purifieth himself, even as he is pure.*

---

[1] See the words of Jesus in Mark 11:33.

The glorious church Jesus is returning for will be one that has accepted the challenges of the devil and is running over him. It will not be a sick and anemic church trying to hold out until the end. You do not find that kind of church in the pages of Scripture. No, it will be a glorious church accomplishing its assignment in a most majestic fashion, reaping the harvest fields in every corner of the globe. And we are that church! That's right! We're the church the gates of hell cannot prevail against about which Jesus spoke of in Matthew 16:18! We're the end-time church Jesus is sending, with His power, into the highways and byways of our world. It is my hope that after you have finished reading this book, you will be more fervent about getting the job done! The harvest of souls is the priority of every believer.

Personally, I have had the good fortune of growing up in the Church. When I was seven, my parents were both marvelously born again, so we began attending church as a family. In every service a statement was made that proclaimed, "Jesus is coming soon! He may come any minute now!" We heard it in the songs we sang, and in every testimony that would invariably conclude with, "And thank God, Jesus is coming soon."

The pastor would enter the pulpit for his sermon, and regardless of what text he read or what message the Holy Spirit had given him, somewhere in that message, at least three times, he would tell us, "Jesus is coming soon — He may come any minute now."

As I grew from childhood to adolescence, they were still saying, "Jesus is coming soon — he may come any minute now." When I became a teenager, they were still saying it. And when I became a young adult, they were *still* declaring it!

So you can understand how keeping that fact in front of us every service affected the way we walked, the way we talked, and the way we won souls. Jesus' soon coming motivated us to soul winning and affected our relationship with one another, as we excitedly anticipated the event. In fact, the coming of Jesus was heralded so emphatically that we actually looked for the event daily.

BE READY

The Bible exhorts us not only to be ready for the appearing of Jesus, but to be looking for it. (Luke 21:28; Hebrews 9:28.) Nevertheless, in recent years I have heard a few preachers say there was no teaching of the catching away of the Church before 1830. Perhaps you've also heard that statement. If you have, let me remind you that Paul taught this truth long before 1830. Ancient manuscripts housed in England reveal that they fervently preached the glorious appearing of Jesus for the express purpose of catching away the Church in both the second and third centuries.

So it is strange that voices today put down the teaching, saying the catching away of the Church is something rather new and isn't going to occur. The Bible not only clearly supports the event, it also reveals when it will occur in relation to the seven years of tribulation.

The church in which I grew up continually expected Jesus' return on any given day. We were constantly told that Jesus was coming soon, but we had no prophetic support for that truth. There would be no prophetic support for "Jesus Is Coming *Soon*" until the birth of Israel in 1948.

Why then was the statement so common? The answer is simple: the Bible reveals the event. But not only that, Jesus and Paul urge all believers to get ready for the event and to stay ready. (Luke 21:28; Titus 2:13; Hebrews 9:28.)

THE FIG TREE BLOOMS

In 1948, when I was twenty-four, something of great importance suddenly occurred. David Ben Gurion, the modern leader of the nation of Israel who would later become its first prime minister, announced on May 14 that the government of Israel would begin to function once again. Then on May 15, the government of Israel began to function for the first time since the sixth century BC, in an Opera House in Tel Aviv. After a period of time in excess of 2550 years the nation of Israel, suddenly began again. With the return of the nation of Israel, prophecies pertaining to the season of Jesus Christ's appearing entered the process of fulfillment.

Today, the prophecies identifying the season of Jesus' appearing are escalating at a very rapid pace. *Jesus is coming soon.* Every believer should be looking for Him. We must allow this truth to have a profound effect on family relationships and relationships with one another as followers of Jesus Christ. The thought of Jesus coming soon should affect the way one helps to propagate the Gospel and the reaching of many souls to bring them into the kingdom of God.

PROPHECY PROCESS

Since 1948, one prophecy after another has entered into the process of fulfillment. When a prophecy enters the fulfillment process, it has only just begun its fulfillment and the process continues over the time God has allotted it. Many fail to understand this.

For instance, when I was a boy, we were taught the prophecies of Joel 2:28,29 which were prophesied some six hundred years before the birth of Christ were completely fulfilled in the first century as recorded in Acts 2:4. We were taught when the 120 initially received the infilling of the Holy Spirit, the prophecy was complete. The truth of the matter is, that was not the prophecy's fulfillment — it was only the beginning. When one carefully examines Joel 2, it becomes clear that only today can the major fulfillment of his prophecies get under way.

Joel's prophecy reads, **And it shall come to pass....** When God says it shall come to pass, whatever He has associated with that term within His book is more certain to come to pass than the rising and setting of the sun.

The mighty God, even the LORD, hath spoken, and called the earth from the rising of the sun unto the going down thereof. —PSALM 50:1

Think about that. Do you ever give a thought as to whether the sun is going to rise or set? So when reading a Scripture and it declares, **It shall come to pass...** pay close attention to whatever God has associated with that statement and realize it will happen — without question.

Again, notice in the opening phrase of Joel's prophecy in verse 28. He uses the term, *afterward,* denoting a series of events — **It shall come to pass** ***afterward.*** Peter didn't use the word "afterward" when he reiterated the prophecy to the great crowd drawn by the upper room experience in Acts 2:16-21.

Peter said, **And it shall come to pass in the last days....** where Joel had written *afterward.* So Peter, unlike Joel, was able to give us a time frame in which this prophecy would be fulfilled. Joel could prophesy the event in its proper chronological order, but he couldn't give the time frame because it was not yet time for the prophecy to be fulfilled. Once the prophecy of Joel began its fulfillment process in the upper room, the Holy Spirit could give Peter the time frame for its total fulfillment — the "last days."

So the major part of Joel's prophecy couldn't be fulfilled until the nation of Israel had come back into national existence, as is stated in Joel 2:18-27. On May 14, 1948, the period began in which Joel's prophecy could be totally fulfilled.

Now let us consider some recent church history to discern our present place in God's plan. In 1948, the Salvation, Divine Healing Crusades were under way across our nation. This was the wave of the Holy Spirit that propelled Oral Roberts and T.L. Osborne into prominence, along with many other men. I also had a canvas cathedral in those days, though not nearly as big as Oral's. It would accommodate several thousand people.

How wonderful was the moving of the Holy Spirit which emphasized salvation and divine healing. Then when that wave of the Spirit seemed to diminish, along came a second wave. (There's always another wave coming in, so don't despair.) The second wave of the Spirit produced the Full Gospel Businessmen. At their peak in the late '60s and through the '70s, the Full Gospel Businessmen were reaching multitudes of men from all walks of life. They introduced them to the saving knowledge of Jesus as well as the Baptism in the Holy Spirit.

When that wave of the Holy Spirit peaked, another wave began to roll in. By the early '60s, it became known as the Charismatic Renewal.

As that wave reached its crescendo and began to break over, another wave rolled in identified as the Word of Faith.

One wave after another. I am so privileged to have lived during this amazing age. Now I declare, based on the authority of God's Word, that there is currently another wave of the Holy Spirit beginning to build. It will continue building to intensity until it reaches a greater height than any of the previous ones. I call this wave the "End-time Harvest". Souls are the object of this wave of the Holy Spirit, and it is now underway. This wave is just one more confirmation that the outpouring of the Holy Spirit prophesied by Joel which began ten days after the glorious ascension of our Lord Jesus Christ — is continuing.

The prophecy of Joel began its fulfillment process in the upper room, and the fulfillment continues to this day. The greatest day of the Church has dawned. It is here now! So as you continue to read the following pages, consider the work of the Holy Spirit and become all the more personally involved in the harvest. The Church has now entered its greatest day in the fulfillment of the long-anticipated appearing of Christ.

CHAPTER 2

THE LAST DAYS

THE LAST DAYS

The frame of time in which the prophecy of Joel 2:28-32 will be fulfilled is known as *the last days.* The initial outpouring of the Holy Spirit is recorded in the Book of Acts, chapter 2. Joel's prophesied last days will include the remainder of the Church Age and the concluding seven years known as the Tribulation.

As you carefully study the prophecies of Joel, you discover that the Holy Spirit will remain here on earth during all seven years of the Tribulation. He will continue conducting His majestic work as it is described in the Scripture.

Many believe the Holy Spirit will be removed before the Tribulation to make way for the Antichrist. But that simply isn't true. Such teaching is traditional theology and is not biblically sound. The Holy Spirit will remain on earth during the Tribulation because the Holy Spirit is God the Holy Ghost, and He is omnipresent. So you just don't take Him out and put Him in. The Holy Spirit has the same characteristics as God the Father and God the Son.

AND IT SHALL COME TO PASS AFTERWARD...

Reading Joel 2:28-32, one discovers that the outpouring of the Holy Spirit which began in the upper room more than 1900 years ago is to continue right up until the day of Jesus Christ's judgmental return when the sun will become black and the moon will be turned red as blood. These two phenomena of nature's upheaval will occur on the final day of the Tribulation. We know this by the statement Jesus made in Matthew 24:29 when He said, **And *after* the tribulation of those days shall the sun be darkened, and the moon shall not give her light.**

Revelation 6:12 confirms Matthew 24:29:

And I beheld when he had opened the sixth seal, and, lo, there was a great earthquake; and the sun became black as sackcloth of hair, and the moon became as blood.... —REVELATION 6:12

You will also discover in John's revelation a major list of massive upheavals of nature that take place on the day of the wrath of the Lamb — Jesus. The day of the wrath of the Lamb is the last day of the Tribulation period.

So throughout the seven year period of tribulation, the Holy Spirit will be here on earth, conducting a massive harvest of souls. He will strongly oppose the Antichrist and everything Satan assigns him to do. I wish someone had taught me this when I was growing up in the Church. If they had, I wouldn't have been as frightened of the Antichrist as most of us were in those days.

Today, we hear much about the Antichrist on Christian television. And from what some of these television prophecy teachers have been saying, you would think he must be just around the corner, and that everything he is going to use is in place.

It is true that everything the Antichrist is going to need and use is here, such as television, radio, electronic technology, computers and computer chips. But this technology and equipment are not evil of themselves. And until the Antichrist is revealed, we must use the same technology to the glory of God.

THE 666 SCARE

Back in the early '70s, a book appeared in Christian bookstores entitled, *666 and When Your Money Fails*. In this book, the author pointed out that the mark of the beast was already here and that it could be found in the bar-codes at the supermarket and on every tag on the pieces of clothing in your favorite store. Many who purchased the book believed the story.

But there is no mark of the beast on anything in this world today. When one studies the Book of Revelation, they discover that the mark of the beast isn't even introduced until the middle of the Tribulation by the false prophet (not by the Antichrist). And by that time, the church company will have already been in heaven for three and a half years.

We live in a marvelous hour in which the fulfillment of the latter day prophecies of Scripture are progressively coming to pass. The rebirth of the nation of Israel in May of 1948 began a series of prophetic events entering into the process of fulfillment. And remember, when one prophecy enters the process of fulfillment, it will continue only so long before it triggers the next prophetic event. Then that prophetic event enters the process and continues for a period of time, triggering yet another prophetic event thus creating a domino effect. It is because of this effect that I can declare we are in the season of His appearing, and that it could take place at a moment's notice.

THE SEASON IS PASSING

Have you given any thought to our calendar? It presently shows us to be in the year 1998. But our calendar is reportedly incorrect. Scientists who study these things tell us it is off by four or five years. They also say they don't know whether we make the correction on the backside of 1998 or the frontside of 1998.

If one makes the correction on the backside of 1998, this is only 1994 or 1993.

If the correction is made on the front side, it's already the year 2002 or 2003.

Regardless, either way they're close. But have you given thought to the fact that should the Lord tarry until January 1 of the year 2000, you and I, will have witnessed the ending of a millennium? Not a century, not a decade, but a millennium.

With the year 2000, we will have passed from the sixth millennium into the seventh millennium according to our INCORRECT calendar. That's close. Realize there have only been five other generations in the history of mankind who have witnessed the ending of one millennium and the beginning of the next. You will be number six.

As the season of Jesus Christ's appearing swirls around us, everyone must get their lives totally in order with God, and so remain. No one can afford to be a fence sitter. No one can afford to be lukewarm, allowing the attitude of the carnal Christian to become their attitude. As we face the end of one millennium and the beginning of the next, we are without question in the season of His appearing. Jesus is coming soon!

Think with me. Should Jesus, by the will of the Father, not come for the Church between now and the year 2000, then shortly after the year 2000, God must send Him.

Why?

A day with the Lord is as a thousand years. Genesis records two thousand years, a two-day period, from Adam to Abraham. Then another two thousand year period from Abraham to Jesus, making four. Then from

32

the first coming of Jesus to establish the Church until His return to the earth to reign (not the catching away of the Church which comes before His return to the earth) is another 2000 year period, making a total of six millenniums. And the Scripture only allows one more millennium — the Seventh Millennium — which will enclose the thousand year reign of Christ here on the earth in absolute peace and righteousness.

A MARKED GENERATION

So we are a marked generation. Have you ever thought about that? You could have been born thousands of years ago, or even one or two generations ago, which would have prevented you from being a part of today's scene. But that wasn't the case. You are here to witness the greatest hour of the fulfillment of Bible prophecy in all of history. Today is the greatest Bible day ever. You are living in the end-time of the last days that will culminate with the appearance of Jesus to catch His church away. There are no past Bible days that can even begin to compare with these days. Are you making the most of them?

CHAPTER 3

CONSIDERING THE FIG TREE

CONSIDERING THE FIG TREE

We are without question in the season of Christ's appearing. These are the final harvest days for souls before our church age ends. But for there to be an end, there had to be a beginning. Jesus is both, Alpha (Beginning), and Omega (Ending).

When Jesus was born of the virgin Mary, the event fulfilled the 700 BC prophecy of Isaiah 7:14. At that time there wasn't nearly as much prophecy being fulfilled as there is today.

When Jesus carried forth His miracle ministry, was arrested, crucified, rose from the grave, and then ascended into heaven to sit at the right hand of His Father, it was a marvelous prophesied period of events. But there wasn't nearly as much prophecy being fulfilled at that time as there is today.

When the Holy Spirit was poured out on the 120 in the upper room, that too was a prophesied event. But there wasn't as much prophecy being fulfilled then as there is in the process of fulfillment today. Today's prophetic events make this the most outstanding Bible day of history.

So if you have ever thought, "Oh, how wonderful it would have been to have lived in Bible days," hit the reject button on your mental computer, kick that out, and reprogram yourself to say, "How wonderful it is to be alive in Bible days."

THE "PROTO EVANGELUM" (FIRST GOSPEL)

Consider this: the Old Testament begins with the first prophetic utterance of God in Genesis 3:15 which was spoken to the serpent after he had beguiled Eve. God prophesied, **The seed of this woman will bruise your head.** There's the prophecy. Did it happen immediately? No. God left the devil in four thousand years of misery awaiting the fulfillment of the prophecy.

So four thousand years passed from the time God prophesied, **The seed of this woman will bruise your head.** And what do you find Satan attempting throughout the Old Testament for those four thousand years? You find him struggling to cut off the seed of the woman.

Satan, however, consistently failed. When the seed of the woman, Who would bring about the fulfillment of God's first prophecy (proto evangelum) came on the scene, He bruised Satan's head. And He did it permanently, Jesus is His name! Therefore, you and I do not have to bruise Satan's head; we only have to maintain his bruise through the enabling Holy Spirit and the Word of God.

THE INSTRUCTIVE POWER OF PROPHECY

The fulfillment of God's first prophecy teaches us several important truths. First of all, it teaches us that prophecy does come to pass, and also that Satan is a master failure. For one to allow Satan to dictate their course in life is tantamount to joining the loser and become an absolute failure. We have discovered that the Old Testament began with a prophetic act — and ends with sixteen prophetic books. The message of prophecy is found throughout the Old Testament.

The New Testament begins with a fulfilled prophecy, the birth of Jesus, Who would bruise the serpent's head and conquer sin. It ends with the majestic book of Revelation that shows an age in which there will be no more sin.

So the prophecies of the Scripture are of utmost importance to us. This is one of the reasons Satan hates the prophecies and has done his best to keep many in a state of confusion concerning them. The apostle Paul writes in 2 Timothy 3:16-17: **All scripture** [that's everything from Genesis 1:1 to Revelation 22:21] **is given by inspiration of God, and is profitable for doctrine, for reproof, for correction, for instruction in righteousness, that the man of God may be perfect, thoroughly furnished unto all good works.**

Based on the above Scripture, we learn that one can never become fully mature or properly equipped for the work that God intends them to do by remaining ignorant of the prophecies of the Scripture. No one can become a full grown mature child of God by ignoring one-third of God's book simply because the major subject is prophecy. Nor can such a person ever be fully equipped to serve God. To take issue with these statements is to declare that the Word doesn't mean what it says.

THE FIG TREE HARVEST

Now let us examine Luke 21:29-33. In this prophetic passage, Jesus addressed the fig tree and all the trees. But first we must understand that Jeremiah established the fig tree as a biblical symbol of Israel in chapter 24 of his book.

> *Thus saith the LORD, the God of Israel; Like these good figs, so will I acknowledge them that are carried away captive of Judah, whom I have sent out of this place into the land of the Chaldeans for their good.*
>
> *For I will set mine eyes upon them for good, and I will bring them again to this land: and I will build them, and not pull them down; and I will plant them, and not pluck them up.* —JEREMIAH 24:5-6

Therefore, the other trees must represent other nations. So another evidence that we are in the season of His appearing is the many nations presently involved in prophetic events.

Today, more than forty nations are actively involved in the fulfillment of Scripture as a result of the fig tree prophecy's process of fulfillment which began in 1948. Israel is one of them, of course. On that same fifteenth day of May, 1948, the combined Arab world declared war on the tiny nation of Israel which wasn't even one day old. That catapulted Israel's war of independence which, by the way, they miraculously won without an army. All

41

Israel had were their guerrilla fighters with which they had resisted the British after World War II during the British mandate of the Holy Land. When the British mandate came to an end on May 14, 1948, the new nation of Israel, under David Ben Gurion, began to function on May 15, 1948.

Today with the exception of Egypt, Jordan, and the PLO, the rest of the Arab world is still officially in a state of war with the nation of Israel.

ISAAC AND ISHMAEL: ANCIENT FAMILY ENEMIES

Consider this fact: the Israelis and the Arabs are blood kin. Both races are descended from Abraham. The Israelis, the Jewish race, came through Isaac and Jacob. The Arab races came through Ishmael. And ever since their births, the world has been observing a four thousand year old family feud over land.

When Jesus said, "Consider the fig tree and all the trees," He posed the question, "Are there other nations involved?"

Absolutely! In 1948, our nation became involved in the fulfillment of the prophecies of the Scripture. It came about when President Harry Truman said to David Ben

Gurion and the nation of Israel, "Come, I'll walk you into the United Nations and see to it that you are seated within this company of nations." At that moment, the United States picked up its major prophetic assignment: becoming the official sponsor of the nation of Israel. Since then, I have listened carefully to everyone of our presidents renew our sponsorship of the nation of Israel. This role brings our nation under the canopy of God's Abrahamic blessing.

Genesis 12:3 states, "Abram, they that bless you, I will bless." And because we have blessed him, we live in the most blessed nation on the earth. If you don't believe me, buy yourself a round-trip ticket in any direction. You won't be away too many days before you will be looking forward to getting back to good old U. S. of A. with all of its problems and occasional chapters in our history book that we would rather have not written.

There is no other place like America. I am fortunate to be able to travel the whole world. I have traveled in Africa, in the Orient, Southeast Asia, Australia and New Zealand, throughout Europe, and in South and Central America. I have offices in Canada, as well as Texas, and I tell you there's just no place like these United States. So be careful lest you allow some liberal politician or confused journalist to influence your attitude against our United States.

Not only are Israel, the United States and all the Arab nations in the process of bringing about fulfillment of the Scriptures, there are others. Russia became involved in the fulfillment of Scripture in 1956 when they went to Egypt's aid against Britain, France, and Israel over the Suez Canal. I remember that event as it brought Russia into the Middle East for the first time in history as the Scriptures prophesy in Ezekiel 38.

Are there yet others? Yes. The nations that make up the common market are now involved in the fulfillment of our current season of His appearing's prophecies. The common market took root in 1957 when six European nations came together to form the European Economic Community (EEC). Today it numbers thirteen, as is prophesied in Daniel chapters 7 and 8, and Revelation 17.

We now have a host of other nations, a host of other trees in bloom, that are carrying out their roles which were prophesied in the Scriptures 2600 to 2000 years ago. They will bring forth the fruits of their individual prophetic fulfillments along with Israel until the season of their purpose in God's end-time harvest is full.

CHAPTER 4

THE NATURE
OF THINGS

CHAPTER FOUR

THE NATURE OF THINGS

Remembering again that Jesus stated in Luke 21:29: **Consider the fig tree and all the trees....** and that Jeremiah identifies Israel as the fig tree in chapter 24 of his book, we have considered the nation of Israel and many other trees, or nations. Jesus went on to discuss the trees as a little nature study, so to speak. So let's follow His nature study to learn more about these trees.

When trees are already budding, you know it is the spring of the year. Spring is always followed by the season of Summer, preceding harvest-time. So Jesus used earth's natural seasons to bring us a biblical truth. Today, we are in a time in which the other trees (nations) He referred to are developing as never before in history, establishing a spiritual season.

For quite some time, a long list of third world countries has existed. That list is now shrinking because many of those former third world countries are becoming highly industrialized and modern. And the world bank is removing them from the third world countries list.

Indonesia is no longer a third world country. Neither are Malaysia, Mongolia, or Singapore. In fact, the once third world city of Singapore has no equal in the United States. It is magnificently beautiful and its laws are enforced.

Today, more than forty nations are actively involved in the fulfillment of the Scriptures. As time progresses, you will hear of other nations that have moved from the category of the third world because of their industrialization and modernization. Such will be the process for a number of the fifteen republics that formerly made up the Soviet Union. Since the fall of Communism and the collapse of the Soviet Union, the outside world rapidly discovered that Russia and her smaller republics were at best third world countries. They possessed first class armies, but were third world in every other respect.

So consider, through His use of seasons of the year to illustrate time frames, Jesus identified the season of His appearing. As nations develop in His parable, it is tantamount to the budding of the "other trees." Jesus prophesied, "when you see these things coming to pass, know you are in the season of My appearing."

So likewise ye, when ye see these things come to pass, know ye that the kingdom of God is nigh at hand.

Verily I say unto you, This generation shall not pass away, till all be fulfilled. —LUKE 21:31-32

With the rebirth of Israel in 1948, the Church took note of the word *generation*. And many assumed forty years made a generation, so they calculated that by 1988 — forty years from 1948 — Jesus would return to the earth to reign. And that seven years before that, the catching away of the Church would occur in 1981.

It never happened, because they didn't understand God's process of prophetic fulfillment. Jesus did prophesy a general time-frame of a generation that wouldn't pass away before His appearing. It would start with the budding of the fig tree, typical of Israel.

Because of Israel's rebirth, our generation has an actual starting date. That date is May 15, 1948. But you can't make this a generation of forty years, because the backside is determined by the fulfillment of all things.

This generation will by no means pass away until *all* things take place. So we have a season. We do not know the day, the hour, the week, the month or the year of the appearing of Jesus, but we do know the season. And we are presently living in it.

To date, we have witnessed fifty years of this season. And in only a few years, regardless of how you approach it, this millennial period is going to be history as a new millennium gets underway.

For those of us who know Him, we can greatly rejoice, because Jesus is coming soon. It could happen at a moment's notice! We are living in the season of His appearing!

CHAPTER 5

HOSEA ON THE
TIME OF OUR SEASON

HOSEA ON THE TIME OF OUR SEASON

For further proof that we are currently living in the season of Jesus' soon appearing, let's consider the Old Testament prophecies of Hosea.

In Hosea's day, the people of Israel were in captivity. Their spiritual backsliding, idolatry, and general rebellion against God swept them into foreign captivity. The ten northern tribes were taken into Assyrian captivity between the years of 721 and 713 BC (933-721 212 years). The two southern tribes that made up Judah (933-606 327 years), existed 115 years longer and were swallowed up by the Babylonian empire between the years of 608 to 586 BC. So in Hosea's day, both the northern and southern kingdoms of Israel had ceased to exist.

Hosea's prophecy begins in 6.1 of his book by calling on Israel to return to the Lord, from whom they had turned away. Then he continues: **for he hath torn, and**

he will heal us; he hath smitten, and he will bind us up.

Please notice this action. Hosea prophesies that Israel had been torn and stricken, but that it wasn't permanent, because next he says: **After two days will he revive us: in the third day he will raise us up, and we shall live in his sight.** The prophecy declares that God will revive Israel in the third day that they may live in His sight. The third day is the one thousand year reign of Jesus. Therefore, the two days represent a two thousand year period.

Let me explain. Under the rulership of the Babylonians, Persians, Greeks, and the Romans, the Israelis were in captivity. Nevertheless, under the authority of these foreign powers, they fared reasonably well. Daniel was made governor of the Babylonian empire under Nebuchadnezzar. Later, he became the first president under the Persian kings, answering only to the king. Judah continued to fare quite well under the Greeks because of that empire's desire to culturally assimilate all of their conquered world.

During the Roman Empire, Caesar gave Judah a half-Jewish king by the name of Herod. So they were still faring reasonably well. However, when God sent their Messiah, and they rejected Him as Isaiah prophesied; the process of being torn and stricken began. To this day no race has suffered at the hands of other people as the Jewish race.

In the eleventh century, the Crusaders marched across Europe under the banner of the cross on their way to liberate the Holy Land from the heathens. While they marched across Europe, they slaughtered thousands of members of the Jewish race — causing Jews to believe that Christians hate them.

Then in the fifteenth century, the Roman Church, which had its own army (and I don't recall this to be unkind to the Roman Church), sent their army into Spain to conduct the Spanish Inquisition. At that time, masses of Jewish people had immigrated to Spain and had come to call the country the second Zion. They were faring very well, and Spain was blessed by their presence. The Spanish Inquisition was designed, as they said, to rid the Church of heretics. Amazingly, they also slaughtered Jewish people by the tens of thousands until they drove them out of Spain.

Many Jewish people who weren't executed or driven out during the Spanish Inquisition took Spanish names

55

to escape annihilation. Then King Ferdinand and Queen Isabella issued a decree at the height of the Inquisition in 1492 which stated from that time forward, no Jewish person could set foot on Spanish soil. This decree stood in place until a few years ago. In 1992 we celebrated the 500th anniversary of the coming of Columbus. It was only then that King Juan Carlos lifted the ancient decree — 500 years after its fifteenth century acclimation!

When the Jews were driven out of their second Zion, they had no place to go. So again they were scattered around the world and persecuted severely. But just as the decree of the Spanish king and queen forbade Jews from living on Spanish soil...Christopher Columbus came on the scene. Columbus was backed by the same king and queen, and set sail on a voyage that would discover the new world. His discovery would provide the next "home away from home" for the Jewish people.

What an amazing development! The prophet Joel stated the nation of Israel would be torn and stricken, and down through the ages history has recorded it. Remember the holocaust? Much is said about Hitler's World War II German holocaust, but not too much has been said about the Russian holocaust. Stalin killed thousands of Jewish people during his despotic purge.

Spiritually backslidden, rebellious Israel had turned from God to idolatry. These conditions led to their being torn and stricken. But God also prophesied to His chosen, "I will heal you and bind you up." Again, the healing process began May 15, 1948. And despite numerous "failed" attempts by Arab forces backed by Russia to exterminate the Jewish race, Israel stands today supremely in the Middle East.

AFTER TWO DAYS...

When considering Hosea's plea: **Come, and let us return unto the LORD: for he hath torn, and he will heal us; he hath smitten, and he will bind us up. After two days will he revive us...,** we must also consider the two-day timeframe prophesied after which God would, heal Israel's wounds. Taking this into consideration, it becomes plain that Hosea's two days equate to two periods of one thousand years. Or, after a two thousand year period, in fact, the same two thousand year period in which the Church has been established and Jesus has been celebrated here on planet earth — Israel will be restored from their torn condition. **In the third day** [after He has revived us] **he will raise us up, and we shall live in his sight.** This would place the

57

third day after the end of our present millennium, during Jesus Christ's one thousand year earthly reign.

Every reference on verse 2 pinpoints the thousand year reign of Christ here on the earth when He will rule over Israel. At that time the nation will be living totally restored in His sight. Hosea's two day period covered the fifth and sixth millennium's since mankind's creation. And that seventh thousand year period is about to begin.

You and I are witnesses to the beginning of God's healing process in Israel. Following our rapture, we will also be witness to their national revival during the Messiah's Millennial reign. We will witness it because Paul prophesied in Romans 11:25-26, that once the fullness of the Gentiles are brought in, all of Israel shall be saved.

For I would not, brethren, that ye should be ignorant of this mystery, lest ye should be wise in your own conceits; that blindness in part is happened to Israel, until the fulness of the Gentiles be come in.

And so all Israel shall be saved: as it is written, There shall come out of Sion the Deliverer, and shall turn away ungodliness from Jacob.... —ROMANS 11:25-26

A major salvation of the Jewish race will come after the catching away of the Church. Salvation is certainly available today, and a small percentage of the world's Jewish population has become Messianic Jews. But God is not yet through with them. During the Tribulation period, they are all going to be saved. Then during the thousand year reign of Christ, their nation will be totally restored in all of its grandeur under Jesus, just as Hosea prophetically said.

So concerning the season of His appearing, Joel's typology of two millennium's that would pass before the restoration of the Jewish people, and Jesus' prophetic blooming of the fig tree shows that we are living in the season.

Isaiah 56 also declares how God will prophetically restore the people of Israel, but adds a reference to the gathering of the Gentiles.

> *The Lord GOD which gathereth the outcasts of Israel saith, Yet will I gather others to him, beside* [not just the outcasts of Israel] *those that are gathered unto him.* —ISAIAH 56:8

This reference certainly places us in a time of harvest — a soul harvest greater than any the world has

ever witnessed. It was prophesied earlier by Isaiah in
chapter 2, verse 2 of his book; by Micah in 4:1; by Jesus
in Luke 14:16-24; and by Paul in Romans 11:25.

*And it shall come to pass in the last days,
that the mountain of the LORD's house shall be
established in the top of the mountains, and shall
be exalted above the hills; and all nations shall
flow unto it.* —ISAIAH 2:2

*But in the last days it shall come to pass, that
the mountain of the house of the LORD shall be
established in the top of the mountains, and it
shall be exalted above the hills; and people shall
flow unto it.* —MICAH 4:1

*And the lord said unto the servant, Go out into
the highways and hedges, and compel them to
come in, that my house may be filled.* —LUKE 14:23

*For I would not, brethren, that ye should be
ignorant of this mystery, lest ye should be wise in
your own conceits; that blindness in part is
happened to Israel, until the fulness of the
Gentiles be come in.* —ROMANS 11:25

These Old and New Testament references clearly
reveal that just before the catching away of the Church,

there is going to be the greatest spiritual awakening of all time. Such an awakening will produce a massive harvest of souls from every race and walk of life. It will surpass all previous harvests of souls, and we are living in the season!

You should know that God has never lost a round in the fight with Satan. So when it comes to the soul count, He will win by a large majority!

Isaiah and Micah come together in excellent harmony in their prophecies which declare, **In the last days *it shall come to pass* that the kingdom of the LORD's house shall be established above the kingdoms and exalted above the nations and peoples from all nations will flow into it.**

The flow won't be a trickle in some little creek. It will be like the massive Mississippi in flood stages rushing over its banks with such a powerful current that men can do nothing about it until the flood subsides. We know who God is going to use to bring it about. His glorious last days Church! We are here, Lord! Send us! Use us!

LORD SEND US!

The fig tree has bloomed, and so have the other trees as Jesus prophesied in Luke 21 which gives us the

61

assurance that our generation is now living in the season of His appearing. Therefore, we must hold nothing back. We must give God our best from now on. THERE ARE SOULS TO BE WON — and He will help us supernaturally as we strive with excellence to get the job done. Jesus said in Luke 14 that His Father's house will be full. And God's house is a big place. The Book of Revelation reveals God's throne room alone is large enough to house all of the righteous at one time plus one hundred billion angels — in one room — all in bodily form. A glorious scene unfolds in Revelation 4 and 5. Later, other groups will arrive from earth to join us when their season is full.

If you like action, I urge you turn your life completely over to the Lord to become a part of His vast last days soul winning combine.

Why?

Because there will be God-given rewards for those who take part in the end-time harvest of souls which is currently upon us. Anyone who has ears to hear and is in tune with the Holy Spirit knows of the tremendous ingathering of souls currently taking place in the former Soviet Union; in South America; Africa; and here in the United States.

The end-time harvest will grow until the harvest is full. Will you grow with it? Will you go? Please understand, the mission field is outside of your home and your church. Wherever there are unsaved people, a mission field exists.

SOULWINNING: THE PROPHETIC ROLE OF THE BELIEVER

THE PROPHETIC ROLE OF THE BELIEVER

If the prophecies of Jesus already covered weren't enough to confirm the fact that we are currently living within the exciting season of Jesus' appearing, the Book of Daniel also gave a sign confirming our time. Mentioned only briefly in one of the verses of Daniel's closing chapter, the prophet amazingly pinpointed the technology of our day — (before technology existed).

But thou, O Daniel, shut up the words, and seal the book, even to the time of the end: many shall run to and fro, and knowledge shall be increased. —DANIEL 12:4

The Word of the Lord to Daniel in this 500 BC prophecy was to shut up the words of his writing until the time of the end when there would be:

1. An unprecedented ability of global travel.

2. And an explosion of knowledge.

Are we there today? Are we really going to and fro and is knowledge truly increasing? Yes! We are! In fact, knowledge is increasing more rapidly right now in the area of technology in particular than ever before. There has never been an hour like it.

To prove this, just go down and buy a new computer tomorrow. Go ahead, and while you're making the purchase ask the salesperson, "How long will it be before I may have to upgrade?" Then watch his or her reaction. You will see they would rather not have to answer that question. Because the chances are very good that by the time you get your new computer installed, it will be veritably antiquated and in need of a lot of upgrading the very next month.

New technologies in computer capability are moving so rapidly today that your new computer will be comparatively obsolete tomorrow.

...and knowledge shall be increased...

But computers are just one way of knowing the hour we're living in. The same thing is happening with our automobiles. The newest models rolling off the assembly lines today are light years ahead of those produced just ten years ago. It's absolutely amazing.

Two years ago I was looking at a certain car that I recently looked at again. The accessories and convenience gadgets that have been added in just two short years totally astounded me. I had never seen anything like it on an automobile before. One of these gadgets is a new noncollision system installed to prevent rear-end collisions. That's right, a noncollision system! It's designed for those particular situations when a driver may be suddenly distracted by someone in the back seat and turns to say something. It will actually brake the car to a stop if another automobile is stopped ahead of them while their head is turned away from the road. With this technological marvel, you couldn't rear-end anything. And I know there are a few of you reading right now who are thinking, "Boy, my wife, my husband, could use one of those."

For just an extra thousand dollars you can have a computer screen put in your car dash today that will show you exactly where you are on a map. You can even point out on the screen where you need to go, and it will show you the roads that will get you there. And if you run into heavy traffic in major cities, you can program the area into your dashboard to produce a computer generated map that will show you alternate routes. Amazing!

A generation ago, the first computer took up the floor space of a large scientific complex. You can see it today in the Smithsonian Museum in Washington, D.C. Today, the same computing power fits into a calculator the size of an earring. And there is more computing power in the dashboard of a car. So we are definitely living in Daniel's time of the end when knowledge would increase. It's not merely increasing, it's exploding!

...many shall run to and fro... (v.4)

And we are also certainly living in Daniel's prophesied generation that would travel to and fro. Today we can travel the globe in a matter of hours which only two generations used to take months!

I have personally traveled the world many times over the past forty years in fulfilling my calling. And no matter what intercontinental airports I am traveling through, even in third world countries, they are beehives of activity. I can step on a jet in Houston one morning, and step off it on African soil the very next day. To think that it was only ninety years ago that the Wright Brothers made their famous first flight on the North

Carolina shores of Kitty Hawk! It's absolutely amazing. And the Almighty told these truths to Daniel 2500 years ago to show us when the seal on his Book would be lifted and the end could begin.

Today, the seal has been lifted and we have entered the beginning of the end. And as I've preached and written for years, the "time of the end" is not doom and gloom. Doom and gloom doesn't edify you. Some factual prophetic truths may be taught by others in a doom and gloom manner, but because they're taught in that fashion, it doesn't build you up, it only lends itself to fear.

So to me, the "time of the end" simply means T.G.I.F. Or, "Thank God, it's Friday!" Because today we're in the last days of the last days which have been in the process of fulfillment now for nearly two thousand years.

We know the Holy Spirit's outpouring in the upper room in Jerusalem with the 120, was a last days event that began the fulfillment of Joel 2. And today, T.G.I.F., we are finally running out of last days. Just as a week has an end of the week, so does the Church Age. And if you're talking about the last days, you're talking about the Church Age.

The weekend is a busy time, isn't it?

Why?

Because on Friday, people get all their loose ends caught up. Everything they had to do that week is brought to completion before the weekend so they don't have to come back to it on Monday. Workers like a clean break, a change of pace. And that's what we're looking forward to in the Church right now. Because the born-again contingent of Christ's heaven-bound church is currently in its Friday, with an end of the age change coming that will alter life on earth. We're going to be raptured. And it's going to be beyond our ability to comprehend until we are caught up to meet the Lord in the air.

Remember, it was the apostle Paul who told us to "Comfort one another" concerning this coming change (1 Thessalonians 4:18.) In Hebrews 10:25 Paul says, "As you see the day of the Lord approaching, you should assemble yourselves together more and more, and not be like others."

And we know the day of the Lord is approaching through the fulfillment of prophetic events — events that are in the process of being fulfilled even as you read this book. So Paul admonishes the believer, "Assemble yourselves together. Come together more and more and more," not "less and less."

However, I can take you to churches all across the country...and I'm talking about "our" kind of churches...Full Gospel, Word of Faith, Pentecostal churches, that no longer have Sunday night service and scarcely have any mid-week services. Everyone goes to church on Sunday morning and you don't see them again until next Sunday morning. That's not caring for your souls, I'm sorry, that's neglecting your souls. Reducing the number of church services is not the answer.

Paul says, "How shall we escape if we neglect so great a salvation?" So if you're not maintaining your salvation as the Scriptures teach, including sitting under the man God has assigned for your spiritual welfare in the house of God, you aren't seeking first God's kingdom, and His righteousness. As a Christian you need to place more emphasis on your spiritual life than anything else.

You may be thinking right now as you read, "Now, Hilton, you're just being a little hard-nosed." Well, never forget it was Jesus who commanded us in Matthew 6:33 to: **Seek ye first the kingdom of God, and his righteousness....** And this word "seek" is not a weak word that doesn't have any force behind it. It's a powerful word, which means those who seek the kingdom of God will labor and grope to find God's will, and when they find it, they will do it. God's will in this end-time harvest is 100 percent commitment to Christ and soulwinning. Thank God, our Friday has arrived. We've got a real change of pace coming, we've got a trip coming up. But first, we have God's will to fulfill in making ourselves available for His last days work.

Again, once a prophetic event enters the process of fulfillment, it has only begun to be fulfilled. It has only entered its process of fulfillment over whatever amount of time God has allotted it. And that timeframe can be found somewhere in the Scripture in relationship to that prophetic event. But you must also understand that during a prophecy's process of fulfillment, its fulfillment period can either be sped up or slowed down. Right now the prophetic events being fulfilled in our generation are being sped up, there is no exception.

But that doesn't mean God may not slow down the last days events in the process of fulfillment swirling around us a month from now.

Why?

To keep them on His timetable. If events get moving too fast, He will find a way to slow them down. So let's return to the Book of Daniel to read the prophecies surrounding verse 3 that were revealed to the prophet 2500 years ago.

And at that time shall Michael stand up, the great prince which standeth for the children of thy people: and there shall be a time of trouble, such as never was since there was a nation even to that same time: and at that time thy people shall be delivered, everyone that shall be found written in the book.

And many of them that sleep in the dust of the earth shall awake, some to everlasting life, and some to shame and everlasting contempt.

And they that be wise shall shine as the brightness of the firmament; and they that turn many to righteousness as the stars forever and ever.

But thou, O Daniel, shut up the words, and seal the book, even to the time of the end: many shall run to and fro, and knowledge shall be increased. —DANIEL 12:1-4

75

Notice Daniel's chronological order: First, he prophesied a time of trouble such as never was, that would require the special attention of the archangel Michael. Out of that time of trouble, which we now know to be the World War II Holocaust, would come the rebirth of the nation of Israel, which we saw in May 1948 because of the Holocaust and war.

Next, Daniel prophesied the resurrection of the righteous and unrighteous indicating the Holocaust period would lead us right up until the time that "many of those who sleep in the dust in the earth shall awake, some to everlasting life." Now please notice, "Some to shame and everlasting contempt." As I will point out thoroughly in chapter 14, these two resurrections will be separated by some thousand years in time. The unrighteous will be resurrected from out of Hades after the Millennium to face the Great White Throne of Judgment (Revelation 20:5,11-15).

But we know from the teachings of the apostle Paul in 1 Thessalonians 4:16-18 that the righteous will be resurrected at the glorious appearing of Jesus. It will be then that the righteous dead of all the ages, Old Testament and New, are going to be resurrected to everlasting life.

So please notice the chronological order in Daniel 12 of how one event is tied into the next. The Holocaust tied into the rebirth of Israel, and the rebirth of the nation of Israel tied to the glorious appearing of Jesus Christ, at which time He will receive a glorious Church unto Himself. Then Jesus brought us confirmation in Luke 21:28 with the parable of the fig tree (which would occur after the Holocaust) when He said:

> *And when these things begin to come to pass, then look up, and lift up your heads; for your redemption draweth nigh.*

And when we get confirmation of Old and New Testament agreeing with one another, that's as strong as it has to be.

So the Holocaust has come, and the rebirth of Israel too. That ties us to the next major event of the glorious appearing of Jesus for the catching away of the Church, **at which time many of those who sleep in the dust of the earth shall awake, some to everlasting life.**

But before that happens, Daniel prophesied one more event in verse 3 of chapter 12 that pertains exclusively to the Church.

And they that be wise shall shine as the bright-
ness of the firmament; and they that turn many to
righteousness as the stars forever and ever.

Daniel prophesied that **those who are wise shall
shine as the brightness of the firmament** [or heavens].

And the "wise" according to Scripture, are those who
win souls:

The fruit of the righteous is a tree of life; and
he that winneth souls is wise. —Proverbs 11:30

You say, "Now Hilton, you wouldn't indicate, would
you, that if I'm not winning souls, I'm not wise?"

To that I say, "No, Hilton Sutton doesn't say
that...the Bible does."

So now you say, "I don't like that. I have my own way
at looking at things, and everything's gone all right up
to now."

To that I say, "The only real thing that matters at all
is the truth contained in God's Word. And God's Word
says if you're a born-again follower of Jesus Christ, you
are a designated soul-winner."

You can't be a born-again follower of Jesus and not be a soul-winner. Maybe you haven't been doing too much launching out into the deep to throw your nets over the side of the boat, but Jesus said you are a soul winner. So all you need to do is make yourself available, and He will bring in the catch.

Too many believers automatically flinch at the idea of soulwinning when the subject comes up of going door-to-door, or witnessing on the streets. And for some, that is their calling because of varying evangelistic gifts.

But for others, most of us actually, we are called to minister to those placed around us as Jesus directs our paths. And we're not called to do it alone! Because Jesus said, **Come, follow me and *I will* make you fishers of men.** Notice His positive statement, "*I will*...make you fishers...." Do you think Jesus would lie? Of course not! So when Jesus said, "*I will* make you fishers of men," He not only designated you as soulwinner, He also guaranteed your catch. Hallelujah! Now that's good news.

Do you remember what happened when Jesus told Peter in Luke 5 to launch out into the deep — again — after a catchless night — only this time with Him in the boat?

And when they had this done, they inclosed a great multitude of fishes: and their net brake.

And they beckoned unto their partners, which were in the other ship, that they should come and help them. And they came, and filled both the ships, so that they began to sink. —LUKE 5:6,7

And do you remember what Jesus told the disciples in John 4:35?

Say not ye, There are yet four months, and then cometh harvest? behold, I say unto you, Lift up your eyes, and look on the fields; for they are white already to harvest.

As a soulwinner appointed by Jesus, all you really have to do is to "look"...because the Lord has already guaranteed a boat-sinking catch.

And they went forth, and preached everywhere, the Lord working with them, and confirming the word with signs following. Amen. —MARK 16:20

All the "world" is outside your door, and they are waiting to see you shine. As I said, you don't have to go knocking on doors, though some are called to do just that. What you need to start doing, if you haven't already, is start saying every morning, "Good morning, Father, here I am, reporting for duty. I thank You, that You will send someone across my path today, with whom I can share Jesus." And if they don't come across your path that day, get up the next morning and say, "Thank you Father for sending someone across my path today."

Then as you continue to become harvest minded, and become sensitive to everyone who crosses your path every day, you will know by the Spirit what to say when they open their lives in need of answers. Or maybe they will say nothing and the Holy Spirit will speak, "That's the one."

So be ready to give a defense of the Gospel, including your testimony to anyone, every day! Because it's a rare thing when one whom God sends across your path will say, "No," when you ask them to pray.

> *And they that be wise shall shine as the brightness of the firmament; and they that turn many to righteousness as the stars forever and ever.* —DANIEL 12:3

Notice in the second half of this verse that the wise in Daniel's chronology of the end of our age will turn *many* to righteousness — not just a few. What a powerful third verse. Therefore, the prophetic role of the believer at the time God is sparing the Jewish race in order to keep His Word is to win souls and bring many into the kingdom of God.

You have friends, neighbors, relatives, and casual acquaintances all around you, who are still unsaved; being harvest minded will inspire you to start being more sensitive to their needs. It's Friday now in our current season of the Church, so start praying about getting those loose ends tied up.

CHAPTER 7

GOD'S BARBED
WIRE FENCE
AROUND HELL

GOD'S BARBED WIRE FENCE AROUND HELL

For the grace of God that bringeth salvation hath appeared to all men,

Teaching us that, denying ungodliness and worldly lusts, we should live soberly, righteously, and godly, in this present world;

Looking for that blessed hope, and the glorious appearing of the great God and our Saviour Jesus Christ;

Who gave himself for us, that he might redeem us from all iniquity, and purify unto himself a peculiar people, zealous of good works.

These things speak, and exhort, and rebuke with all authority. Let no man despise thee. —TITUS 2:11-15

When I grew up in church I continually heard that multitudes of people were dying and going to hell who had never heard about Jesus. That troubled me, provoking me to think, *God, how can You be just while masses of people are being sentenced to hell without having ever heard?* But I kept hearing it again, and again, and again.

Then one day while I was studying His Book, the Holy Spirit said, "Here is the answer to your dilemma." My biblical dilemma was created by my own lack of knowledge of the Word of God and the fact that I was hearing statements which didn't ring properly within my spirit. So I turned to the verse of Titus cited above. It starts:

> *For the grace of God that bringeth salvation hath appeared to all men....* —Titus 2:11

And after I meditated on it for some time I discovered from the authority of the Word of God that it is utterly impossible for anyone to be born into this world and not have, at some time or another in their life, an opportunity to come to know God's Son, Jesus Christ — utterly impossible!

So on the authority of the Scripture, I want you to know that if you have also happened to hear that masses of people have gone to hell from this life who had no opportunity to hear the Name of Jesus, this is not Bible. Because the Scripture says, **For the grace of God that bringeth salvation hath appeared to all men...**

Teaching us that, denying ungodliness and worldly lusts, we should live soberly, righteously, and godly, in this present world;

Looking for that blessed hope, and the glorious appearing of the great God and our Savior Jesus Christ;

Who gave himself for us, that he might redeem us from all iniquity, and purify unto himself a peculiar people, zealous of good works.

Paul next told Titus in verse 15 to, "Speak these things." Now this is a very powerful statement, and one that every last days designated soulwinner/believer needs to hear. "Speak these things."

It is here that Daniel's 12:3 admonition to the latter days harvest believer **who shall shine as the brightness of the firmament because of turning many to righteousness** should apply to those you know within the Church. You need to be quick to remind those around you of God's holy, righteous ways.

You're not imposing on a fellow Christian when you remind them how we *all* ought to be denying ungodliness and worldly lusts. Or when you remind them how we all need to be living soberly, righteously, and godly in the present age as we look for the blessed hope and glorious appearing of our great God and Savior Jesus Christ. He gave Himself for us that He might redeem us from every unrighteous deed. So you don't need to fear that you will hurt someone's feelings, especially if they're a child of God, when you say, "You need to be about the Master's business."

These things speak, and exhort, and rebuke with all authority. Let no man despise thee. —Titus 2:15

But of utmost importance to our last days calling as soulwinners, we are to know that the grace of God has appeared unto all men, declaring His salvation.

Well now, you may say, "Hilton, what about the hidden people groups around the world that have yet to receive a Christian missionary?"

To that, I say, we have Scripture that tells us even the heavens declare the glory of God.

For the invisible things of him from the creation of the world are clearly seen, being understood by the things that are made, even his eternal power and Godhead; so that they are without excuse.... —ROMANS 1:20

Plus, there is the work of the Holy Spirit. Jesus tells us in John 16:7-11 that when the Holy Spirit comes He will convict the world of sin.

Nevertheless I tell you the truth; It is expedient for you that I go away: for if I go not away, the Comforter will not come unto you; but if I depart, I will send him unto you.

And when he is come, **he will reprove the world of sin....** —JOHN 16:7,8

Therefore, there isn't a person alive who isn't presently under Holy Spirit conviction. And if God has been so precise in previous generations, how much more so in these last days. Because we know it is not the will of God for anyone to be lost, and that all should come to repentance.

The Lord is not slack concerning his promise, as some men count slackness; but is longsuffering to us-ward, not willing that any should perish, but that all should come to repentance. —2 PETER 3:9

Notice this verse in 2 Peter 3:9 doesn't say all *will* come to repentance. It says all *should* come to repentance: because the choice is always with the individual who God is long-suffering toward. Due to the season we are currently living in, the sooner you open your eyes to the harvest, the sooner you will discover **there is a barbed wire fence around hell.**

Now, how did I come by such a thought? I picked it up from a conversation between Jesus and His disciples recorded in Matthew 16 which began when Jesus asked His disciples, **Whom do men say that I am?**

After Jesus asked the question, He received various answers. One of His disciples said others were claiming Jesus was one of the prophets. Others were saying He was Elijah, or Jeremiah. Some even thought Him to be John the Baptist reincarnated. These answers actually indicated the people were grossly involved in the doctrine of devils known as reincarnation.

But when Peter responded, He answered with truth: **Thou art the Christ: the Son of the Living God.** So Jesus said, **Blessed art thou Simon Barjona: for flesh and blood has not revealed this to you, but My Father who is in heaven. And I also say to you that**

you are, Peter.... (which means a *piece of rock,* or a "building stone," not a foundational stone, because there is much difference between the two) "And on this rock..." (the word "rock"[1] here, meaning a *massive rock,* or foundational stone) **"I will build My Church and the gates of hell shall not prevail against it."**

Now notice what Jesus said: **...the gates of hell would not prevail against the church.** When I first received this revelation of hell's barbed wire fence (while traveling around the country with a gospel tent) I thought... *gates?* Then, I thought, if there were gates, there must also be a fence. Because without a fence, gates are absolutely of no benefit. So I asked the Holy Spirit to develop this for me. And when He did, He directed me to Isaiah.

So let me take you now to Isaiah 26:1.

> *In that day shall this song be sung in the land of Judah; We have a strong city; salvation will God appoint for walls and bulwarks.*

This verse has to do with a song of salvation to be sung in God's strong Judean city that would be surrounded by

---

[1] Strong, James, "Greek Dictionary of the New Testament," *Strong's Exhaustive Concordance of the Bible*, Nashville: p. 57, #4074, #4073.

impenetrable, fortress walls. So I quickly learned that the plan of salvation which God Himself magnificently designed, literally serves as the posts for His barbed wire fence around hell. Because God's plan of salvation according to the Word is like a wall and a bulwark.

It's not only God's will that men not perish and be lost, but it is in His plan to go out of His way to keep that from happening if men will give Him the least of their attention.

As I mentioned earlier, in part anyway, the church I grew up in made it difficult for folks to go to heaven, but so very easy to go to hell. We had everybody on the broad path that leads to hell and destruction. And we had it well greased. It was so slippery that we put most everybody outside of the born-again church sliding down on at least one banana peel.

Our pastor would preach: "Many are called but few are chosen!" Emphasis was placed on "the few" so strongly you would think there were only three or four of us. A re-emphasis made you wonder about the other three! And you usually did that while racing down to the altar to rededicate your life.

If anyone just allowed themselves to think of or do the least little thing that wasn't pleasing to God, we immediately branded them with a red hot iron that said, "Backslider!" And the chances were quite good they hadn't even backslid. We were just good about making it so easy to go to hell.

There are probably some folks in hell today that some Christian helped get there, you know, because of being foolish. We didn't use wisdom, because we didn't really know enough of the Word of God. We were not aware of the provisions God had made.

God has created a massively powerful operation to keep men and women out of hell. But that doesn't mean men and women can't eventually go there. If the unconverted persist in their rejection of Jesus and the loving conviction of His Holy Spirit, they send themselves there. There is a straight and narrow way. The Scripture says so in Matthew 7.

> *Enter ye in at the strait gate: for wide is the gate, and broad is the way, that leadeth to destruction, and many there be which go in thereat....* —MATTHEW 7:13

It's just that many in the church made it so straight and so narrow that it was a tightrope stretched across Niagara Falls with the devil on either side shaking it.

But the truth of the matter is, those who have already entered hell, could not have entered until they had bounced off God's barbed wire fence that surrounds it, over, and over again and again!

For example, do you remember the occasion in Acts 9 when a Pharisee of the Sanhedrin, a man of great authority, was given the assignment to persecute the Church? His name was Saul, and while riding on his horse with some others to Damascus one day to apprehend the Church, the Lord apprehended him. When you read the account, you will see that Jesus flashed him off his horse to the ground, then asked him "Why are you persecuting Me? It is hard to kick against the pricks." What He actually said was "Saul, in your zeal to do My will, you are fighting *against* My will." And the rest is Church history, because Saul ran into and bounced back from God's barbed wired fence around hell.

Can you think back to the days before you were born again to remember your brushings against God's barbed wire fence protecting you from hell? Can you remember when He pricked your conscience with one of the barbs of that fence?

For a while you may have said, "Oh, I know I'm not right with God, but one of these days I know I'll change." But then you continued on in sin, all the while in the conviction of God's desire. Why? Because of your brush with the barbs in God's fence.

So hell's barbed wire fence is there...to keep people out, and to keep them from finding hell's gates. Jesus said hell has gates in Matthew 16:18.

Anyone who bounces off God's barbed wire fence around hell again and again throughout their lifetime will eventually come to hell's unlocked gates. And once there, it only takes a little nudge of the devil to send them plunging through the gates and into the abyss, eternally lost and separated from God.

Those who are in hell today, succeeded in bouncing off of God's fence again, and again, until they finally found the gate. And I can assure you that not one of them intentionally plunged through to their eternal doom.

Satan infuses the lost with pride and ignorance that often resists God's barbs and pricks, eventually bringing them to hell. Jesus states that Satan comes but to steal, kill, and destroy! Once he has succeeded in causing one to maneuver through many rejections of the Lord Jesus, he slowly positions them, to finally shove them in.

This is another reason every believer should take up their commission as an officer in Jesus' last days' harvest season soulwinning troop. Because here again, the Lord has ensured the catch of every one of His shining fishers, including a bulwark around the devil's desires.

GOD'S BARBED STRANDS ON HELL'S PROTECTIVE FENCE

You can find the strands of hell's barbed wire fence listed in His Word. The first one is the **blood of the Lamb** as Peter lists it in 1 Peter 1:18,19:

> *Forasmuch as ye know that ye were not redeemed with corruptible things, as silver and gold, from your vain conversation received by tradition from your fathers;*
>
> *But with the precious blood of Christ, as of a lamb without blemish and without spot....*

STRAND 1: THE BLOOD OF THE LAMB

Strand number one is the blood of the Lamb. You've heard it said by many evangelists down through the years, that to leave this world without God, you must trample under your feet the shed blood of Jesus. This is certainly true, because the blood of Jesus has been sprinkled all around hell and is powerfully working as a strand in God's fence to keep people out of it.

Another powerful passage concerning the blood is recorded in Hebrews 10:19:

Having therefore, brethren, boldness to enter into the holiest by the blood of Jesus...

This verse tells us that the blood of Jesus provides us access to God. So the very blood of Jesus that has been shed — which gives us access to God — also keeps us out of hell once we recognize the powerful covenant effect of that blood, as we plunge into it for the remission of our sins.

The blood of Jesus is so powerful that it washes you clean of every sinful stain. When you study the Word of God about the blood of the Lamb, you discover that the flowing of the blood is continuous. The present, perfect cleansing of the blood of the Lamb — you can walk in it every day!

So not only is the blood of the Lamb a powerful strand on God's barbed wire fence to keep folks out of hell, it is by the blood of the Lamb that we are redeemed. And it is by the blood of the Lamb that we remain redeemed! Hallelujah!

We need to constantly remember the crucifixion of our Lord Jesus Christ to thank God for His blood. Roman crucifixion was without a doubt the most tormenting, painful manner of execution ever invented by man. While Jesus endured it, His blood was shed from His pierced hands, feet, brow, and side, as it flowed down to the earth, carrying with its every drop enough power to save the world.

OH, THE BLOOD OF JESUS

I don't hear it much anymore, but I used to hear God's people often say, "I plead the blood."

Why?

Because of its power. I'd hear folks say, "The blood of Jesus covers me and because of the blood of Jesus, Satan, you can't walk through!" All one needs to do is plunge into the blood of the Lamb. The born-again believer is on the right side of His blood, praise God — not the wrong side. The blood of the Lamb will keep us out of hell as we walk in God's light to cleanse us from all sin:

But if we walk in the light, as he is in the light, we have fellowship one with another, and the blood of Jesus Christ his Son cleanseth us from all sin. —1 JOHN 1:7

So the first strand of God's barbed wire fence around hell is the blood of Jesus. No one is ever going to enter into hell without having an encounter with the blood of Jesus, which they must reject in order to pass through hell's gate.

STRAND 2: THE GOSPEL

The second strand on hell's barbed wire fence around hell is the Gospel. You need to know that even those who reject it when you share it with them are influenced by its power. Because the Gospel is powerful. It will prick people's hearts, and keep them out of hell. That's why Paul writes in Romans 1:16 and 17 **...I am not ashamed of the gospel of Christ: for it is the power of God unto salvation to everyone that believeth; to the Jew first, and also to the Greek. For therein is the righteousness of God revealed from faith to faith: as it is written, The just shall live by faith.**

Any man or woman who goes to hell has to reject the powerful Gospel. But you say, "Suppose they don't hear?"

Impossible, because I proved that from Titus 2:11 that is impossible. The Gospel is in creation (Romans 1:18), and today is being preached in unprecedented ways in missions, over radio, and on TV around the world.

Again, you may not be called by God to go into *all* the world, but you do have a call to preach the Gospel to everyone in your neighborhood, at your job, and in your marketplace.

STRAND 3: THE HOLY SPIRIT

Now let's look at the third strand in God's fence around hell — the Holy Spirit. No one can possibly get into hell without encountering the Holy Spirit, because God has sent His Holy Spirit all the way around hell. Jesus explained His coming "placement" in John 16:7-11:

Nevertheless I tell you the truth; It is expedient for you that I go away: for if I go not away, the Comforter will not come unto you; but if I depart, I will send him unto you.

And when he is come, he will reprove the world of sin, and of righteousness, and of judgment:

Of sin, because they believe not on me;

*Of righteousness, because I go to my Father,
and ye see me no more;*

*Of judgment, because the prince of this world
is judged.*

The Holy Spirit is "He" or "Him," the third Person of
the Godhead. Just as much as God is God, the Father is
God, and the Son is God, the Holy Spirit is God. We speak
of Him more as the Holy Spirit. But we sometimes use
that term so commonly, we almost forget Who He really is.

I've often heard it said that God will never violate a
person's will and force them to go His way. That's true,
the Heavenly Father won't do that, but the Holy Ghost
will. He will wake someone up in the middle of the night
and put them under such heavy conviction that they
can't go back to sleep. And in the morning their family
members will wonder what made them so grouchy.

Then there may be other times when someone is
regularly going about their day when suddenly, the Holy
Spirit's conviction just looms right up in front of them,
and just as suddenly — they are miserable! "Why me?"
they might say. "Okay, I'll go to church Sunday."

The conviction of the Holy Spirit is designed to keep folks out of hell. He is the third strand in God's protective barbed wire fence. And like the blood of Jesus, He will keep you in fellowship with Himself in harmony with the truth and conviction of God's written Word.

In verses 13 and 14 of John 16 Jesus said:

Howbeit when he, the Spirit of truth, is come, he will guide you into all truth: for he shall not speak of himself; but whatsoever he shall hear, that shall he speak: and he will shew you things to come.

He shall glorify me: for he shall receive of mine, and shall shew it unto you.

What a powerful work of the Holy Spirit! He keeps men out of hell, and keeps them in God's fold. So be sure to maintain a daily fellowship with Him. Don't let a day go by in which you haven't set aside some time for fellowship with the Holy Spirit. It's wonderful.

Some folks may respond, "Well, I'm not baptized in the Holy Spirit." I'm not writing about the experience of being baptized in the Holy Spirit. I'm referring to the fellowship of the Spirit. Since you met the Holy Spirit when you were born again, you can fellowship with Him. So quit making excuses. You entered into fellowship with the Holy Spirit when you were born again — when the Holy Spirit placed you into Jesus — and Jesus took up residence in you. So you shouldn't have any resistance whatever to any future experiences with the Holy Spirit...especially speaking with other tongues...because as you study the Scriptures, they explain that tongues are of the Holy Spirit.

Thank God for the Holy Ghost who encircles hell with His convicting power, pricking the hearts of men. Every time someone brushes up against the barbs on God's security fence, the Holy Spirit says, "You don't want to do this. Move away. Pay attention to God."

STRAND 4: THE NAME OF JESUS

The fourth strand on God's barbed wire fence that guard's all people from hell, is the Name of Jesus, because Romans 10:13 says:

For whosoever shall call upon the name of the Lord shall be saved.

Can you imagine the chance Satan takes every time he causes someone to brush against hell's fence and they're pricked by the Name of Jesus? He takes the chance that they may cry out at that very moment, "Jesus, be merciful to me! Save me!" And what do you think God does when He hears such a cry? He saves them instantly, right then and there. Because, **Whoever calls on the Name of the Lord shall be saved.** That's what Peter said after receiving a fresh anointing from the Holy Ghost in Acts 4:10-12 when he declared:

Be it known unto you all, and to all the people of Israel, that by the name of Jesus Christ of Nazareth, whom ye crucified, whom God raised from the dead, even by him doth this man stand here before you whole.

This is the stone which was set at nought of you builders, which is become the head of the corner.

Neither is there salvation in any other: for there is none other name under heaven given among men, whereby we must be saved.

So, here again, no one goes to hell without having had an encounter with the Name of Jesus — no one.

Once I was in the presence of someone who was constantly taking the Name of Jesus in vain, when someone turned to me and addressed me as, "Reverend."

When they did, this person said, "You're a preacher?" I said, "Yes." So he said "Oh, my God, I'm sorry!" Every few words this man was saying Jesus this and Jesus that in a vain, profane way. And if one who is using the name of Jesus in vain encounters the Spirit's conviction simply because he realizes he's in the presence of a preacher, how much more the Holy Spirit will convict that one whom Jesus Himself confronts in the power of His name!

Wherefore God also hath highly exalted him, and given him a name which is above every name.

That at the name of Jesus every knee should bow, of things in heaven, and things in earth, and things under the earth... —PHILIPPIANS 2:9-10

Praise God that He has hell fenced in with the name of Jesus! It kept me out. And it kept you out before you could find hell's open gate:

And that every tongue should confess that Jesus Christ is Lord, to the glory of God the Father. —PHILIPPIANS 2:11

The fence God built to keep people out of hell is a testimony to the fact of His great love for people. We have a strong city around which the salvation of God has been appointed for walls and bulwarks.

So we can be absolutely certain by the authority of Scripture that it is not the will of God for a single human being to be lost. If God has surrounded hell with the blood of the Lamb, the Gospel, the Holy Spirit, and the Name of Jesus to restrain earth's people from finding hell's gate, shouldn't those of us empowered with His saving grace do everything in our power to lead them through God's gate?

It's time to work the fields because it is harvest season in the Church. Jesus has not only called us to be last days' fishers, He has also guaranteed a catch to any who will ask Him to send the harvest their way.

Start praying and expecting God's power and mercy to increase in your life. It was mercy that sent Jesus to the cross to keep you out of hell. And it will be mercy that takes you to heaven because His mercy ushered you in. So in the next chapter we will look at the mercy of God from His perspective to add to your inspiration as you grow in your prophetic, soulwinning role.

CHAPTER 8

—JOHN 3:16—
HIS MERCY
ENDURETH FOREVER
GOD'S FOUR PHASES
OF MERCIFUL LOVE

—JOHN 3:16—
HIS MERCY ENDURETH FOREVER
GOD'S FOUR PHASES OF MERCIFUL LOVE

For God so loved the world, that he gave his only begotten Son, that whosoever believeth in him should not perish, but have everlasting life. —JOHN 3:16

Anyone who has ever truly been touched by the saving mercy of God will testify to the heart melting embrace of Jesus Christ's acceptance when they were born again. Then as we grow in the knowledge of the Scriptures, a deeper understanding of God's mercy envelops our lives. The length to which the Father actually went in demonstrating His mercy through the sacrifice of His son is astounding.

Therefore, if you have been born again by the wonderful mercy of God, there ought not to be a human

109

being of your acquaintance that you have no feelings for, in relationship to their salvation. There should not be one lost person of whom you could say, "Oh well, they brought it on themselves. Serves them right." That shouldn't be part of our vocabulary. If God doesn't want people to perish, neither should we! Amen? That means if God's going out of His way to keep people out of hell, you and I should join with Him to do our best to fulfill His will. As you stay faithful, one day they're going to search you out and say, "What is this you've been telling me all these years? Tell me a little more."

First Chronicles 16:34 declares that the mercy of God endures forever. Psalms 105 says His mercy is everlasting. And 2 Peter 3:9 says, **The Lord is not slack concerning his promise, as some...count slackness; but is longsuffering to us-ward....**

Why?

Now look at this: because He is **not willing that any should perish, but that all should come to repentance.**

We can strive, and are able to be like God in our calling as soulwinners because His textbook gives us instructions, and the Holy Spirit is at work within us to be more and more like Him.

Please notice God's Word doesn't say everyone He wants to save *will* come to repentance. It says, they *should* come to repentance. But how will they ever know they need to come to repentance? Someone has to share just enough of God's Word with them, so they understand eternity with God begins with heartfelt repentance.

We currently have a generation of people on our hands in which there are many who have no conscious awareness of God whatsoever. There are a host of '90s folks, in their teens, early twenties, and in their thirties, who don't know repentance is required if they're going to bypass perishing. They never think about God. There's no element of God in anything they do. They are lacking when it comes to the fear of God spoken of in Psalm 111:10 and Proverbs 9:10: **The fear of the LORD is the beginning of wisdom....**

Most people in generations previous to this one grew up knowing that if we were about to do something evil, bad, or wrong — we would think, "I know this is not right, and someday I'll stand before God and give an answer." The thought came often enough to keep us from wrong doing. Such is not so with our present generation. So it is up to the Church, more than ever, to tell them about Jesus to relieve them from the vanity of this life, and to spare them from hell.

For God so loved the world, that he gave his only begotten Son, that whosoever believeth in him should not perish, but have everlasting life. —JOHN 3:16

God has indeed gone His mile and more to provide a way for men and women to partake of His mercy.

You know, it's not difficult to get saved. You can't work your way into it. So there is no regime of mental or physical toil after which, through a sufficient amount of penitence, the goal has been achieved and the reward laboriously achieved. No, the Scriptures say:

For whosoever shall call upon the name of the Lord shall be saved. —ROMANS 10:13

I am convinced there will be a lot of folks in heaven that we never expected to see there. By the same token, there will probably be some folks in hell that we thought would have been in heaven.

Why?

Because they never truly called:

For whosoever shall call upon the name of the Lord shall be saved. —ROMANS 10:13

Once you have called on the Lord to be merciful to you, He accepts you as His child and writes your name in the Lamb's Book of Life. He sets your feet on the solid rock, puts a song in your heart, then teaches you in Scripture to "keep on calling on Him." As a born-again believer, you should never let a day go by that you're not renewing your relationship and enjoying the excitement of walking with the Lord on a daily basis. It is exciting!

How then shall they call on him in whom they have not believed? and how shall they believe in him of whom they have not heard? and how shall they hear without a preacher? —ROMANS 10:14

You should never let a day go by without looking for those opportunities to do some preaching about which I wrote in chapter 6. Everyone who is a born-again child of God has a right to do some preaching, because Jesus' words in Mark 16:15 tell us to: **Go ye into all the world and preach the gospel.**

As a born-again child of God, you've got a Bible right to preach in your neighborhood; to preach in your family; to preach where you work; and to preach where you do business. So be bold in situations when you have a "captive audience." If you believe, and not doubt, God will back you up.

For instance, when traffic gets stopped and you're just sitting there, put your window down, motion to the fellow, and as he rolls his window down, say, "Just wanted to know whether or not you know the Lord Jesus, He loves you, you know?" You may be shocked when he answers back, "Yes, thank you, praise God." I've had this happen to me, so that's the reason I know. Such action, though unusual, can be successful.

It is simply time that we who profess to be believers begin to act and talk like believers and begin to practice what is in God's book. I still continue to this day sitting down with some of my family members, saying to them, "I want to tell you, until you folks get back in church and serve God as you know you should, nothing's going to work right in your life. You need to get in the house of God and serve Him with all your heart, then things will get straightened out."

And things can get straightened out, because of the mercy of God.

GOD'S FOUR PHASES OF MERCIFUL LOVE

The mercy shown God's people should have us looking for every opportunity to thank Him by showing His mercy to others every day, on and off the job. The mercy of God will endure forever. It has endured throughout the ages, just as it will continue throughout the Tribulation and Millennium periods.

You say, "But I've heard God's mercy will cease once the Church is raptured...."

Well, maybe you have, but you've heard wrong. Because everlasting means everlasting:

> *For the LORD is good; his mercy is everlasting; and his truth endureth to all generations.* —PSALM 100:5

MERCY PHASE 1
SOULWINNING THROUGH THE CHURCH

> *For I am not ashamed of the gospel of Christ: for it is the power of God unto salvation to everyone that believeth; to the Jew first, and also to the Greek.* —ROMANS 1:16

Today God shows His mercy through the preaching and demonstration of His good news — the Gospel — through the agency of His Church. It is our responsibility. We should take that responsibility seriously enough to know that our rewards in heaven as believers will be contingent upon how we share God's Gospel of salvation with others right NOW.

So once again, let me say that it's fine for folks to go knocking on doors. If you're a door knocker, I'm all for it! I'm all for going house-to-house, telling people about your church while offering them a publication. I'm all for asking them if they would like to pray! But not everyone can go knocking on doors.

"LORD, USE ME!"

Everyone can, however, pray and say, "Lord, send someone across my path." Then start watching and expecting Him to do it. And as they come, share the Lord Jesus with them — and expect results. Expect results!

Realize that when you pray, "God, send someone across my path with whom I can share the Gospel," you are setting in motion the power of God which is going to deliver them because we have a powerful Gospel that will save everyone who believes.

Now that's part of our expectancy. If we are obeying the Word of God and are sharing His supernatural dynamite, in due course of time, it's going to blow those we share it with out of Satan's clutches, right into the Kingdom of God!

The Church's number one priority right now is the demonstration and preaching of the mercy of God. So we need to check our hearts and come to grips with the reality that we're not ashamed of the Gospel. If you're ashamed of what others may think of the truth, and of you — stop it, because time is short, and Jesus said, **If the world hate you, ye know that it hated me before it hated you** (John 15:18).

The Gospel is the power of God unto salvation. Someone shared it with us until the day we were ready by faith to receive the Gospel truth and said, "Jesus, I need You." And when we said that, He was present immediately.

THE GOSPEL OVERCOMES

Revelation chapter 12:11 says:

And they overcame him by the blood of the Lamb, and by the word of their testimony; and they loved not their lives unto the death.

The Church overcomes the devil not only by the blood of the Lamb that surrounds the gates of hell, but by our personal testimony that we're constantly sharing with others.

I have met a lot of folks who aren't overcoming. They're quick to recognize the blood of the Lamb, but they won't testify. They simply won't tell anyone about Jesus.

I've heard some say, "Well, I'm just afraid of rejection." And, "If I talk about Jesus, I may lose my job." To them I say, pay attention: "If you lose your job because you're talking about Jesus, God will give you a better one!"

It's simply time that we, the people of God, cease allowing the devil and the world to intimidate us. If they can curse out on the public street and in the supermarket, we can say, "Praise the Lord! Glory to God!" If they can take God's name in vain, we can say, "Jesus you are Lord and worthy to be praised! Hallelujah!"

I *refuse* to be intimidated by the government. They aren't going to shut my mouth! I refuse to be intimidated by pseudo-intellectuals. I refuse to be intimidated by the politically incorrect. They're not correct. They talk about political correctness, but they're so confused and fouled up that I wouldn't follow them a half step down the street, much less a block. I refuse to be intimidated by the devil's crowd, and so should you. The "politically correct" need to hear about Jesus! Amen? And if we will allow Him, the Holy Ghost will give us boldness to open our mouth and speak.

You say, "That may get me in trouble."

So what?

God will get you out of any trouble your testimony gets you into. Read God's book! See what He did for Daniel, Shadrach, Meshach, or Abednego! (Daniel 3:12.)

THE GOSPEL EXPLODES

But ye shall receive power, after that the Holy Ghost is come upon you: and ye shall be witnesses unto me both in Jerusalem, and in all Judaea, and in Samaria, and unto the uttermost part of the earth. —ACTS 1:8

The explosive power our Gospel exudes is another reason to act in boldness around the devil's intimidating crowd. Remember, Jesus told His disciples that after the Holy Ghost had come upon the Church we would receive "power," dunamis[1], spiritual dynamite, ability over and beyond human ability to be His witnesses. Jesus said we would be His representatives, in "Jerusalem," that's your hometown; in "Judea," that's your county; in "Samaria," that's your state; and in the "uttermost parts of the earth"; that's anywhere else.

---

[1] Strong, James. "Greek Dictionary of the New Testament," *Strong's Exhaustive Concordance of the Bible*, Nashville: Abingdon, p. 24, #1411.

So whether God allows you to be moved somewhere or if you are to stay at home — you are to be His explosive witnesses in demonstration of the Gospel every day. You are a witness and minister of God's miracle power. And nothing will get the world's attention more than the demonstration of His power.

Remember, Jesus said in Mark 16:15-20:

...Go ye into all the world, and preach the gospel to every creature.

He that believeth and is baptized shall be saved; but he that believeth not shall be damned.

And these signs shall follow them that believe; In my name shall they cast out devils; they shall speak with new tongues;

They shall take up serpents; and if they drink any deadly thing, it shall not hurt them; they shall lay hands on the sick, and they shall recover.

So then after the Lord had spoken unto them, he was received up into heaven, and sat on the right hand of God.

And they went forth, and preached everywhere, the Lord working with them, and confirming the word with signs following. Amen.

Once our assignment of showing God's mercy is finished, the Church will be caught away, the Tribulation will begin, and phase two of God's mercy will immediately commence. Over the course of this phase of God's mercy, multitudes of Jews and Gentiles *will* be saved.

MERCY PHASE 2
SALVATION FOR THE TRIBULATION SAINTS

For I would not, brethren, that ye should be ignorant of this mystery, lest ye should be wise in your own conceits; that blindness in part is happened to Israel, until the fulness of the Gentiles be come in.

And so all Israel shall be saved: as it is written, There shall come out of Zion the Deliverer, and shall turn away ungodliness from Jacob:

For this is my covenant unto them, when I shall take away their sins. —ROMANS 11:25-27

This is a very revealing New Testament passage in which Paul writes "that blindness in part has happened to Israel, until the fullness of the Gentiles be come in." And that "All of Israel will be saved."

When?

After the fullness of the Gentiles has been brought in. When that happens, the stage will be set for all of Israel to be saved in the last possible moments of premillennial history.

We are grateful to God for the Jewish people who are accepting Jesus as their Messiah right now. But do you realize they are few in number, compared to the Jewish population? Today there are Jewish Christian groups all around the country, but they're usually just a small group of believers.

Once the Church is gone, all Israel will be saved says Paul in Romans 11. Everyone who has been born again, baptized in the Holy Spirit, and is following the Lord Jesus Christ at this point, will have been caught away to heaven.

But if you're backslidden and the Rapture occurs, you will stay on earth. Neither will you be caught up with the rest of us if you're a lukewarm Christian like the church of Laodicea in Revelation 3. If this happens to be the case it won't mean you are lost, just that you missed the Rapture, and that you will be going through part of the Tribulation.

Nevertheless I have somewhat against thee, because thou hast left thy first love. —REVELATION 2:4

If you're reading this chapter and you have been taking the grace of God in vain (See 2 Corinthians 6) with one foot in the world, and the other in church, wake up! Keep in mind that the Lord Jesus and the apostle Paul both taught that we must be in a state of readiness for the Rapture. Read carefully Matthew 25:1-13 and Revelation chapters 2:1-7 and 3:14-22, and you will see how important it is not to let a day go by that we don't make sure our salvation is right up to date. Don't allow yourself the ordeal of coming back to the Lord as a Tribulation saint. Though, we can certainly thank God for the merciful opportunity.

TEN-TO-ONE MERCY

I know this truth destroys the teaching that declares only Jews will be saved during the Tribulation. All Israel will be saved, but Zechariah 8:23 says, **During that time there will be ten men of other nations, in other words, Gentile men, that will come to him**

who is a Jew, and say, We have heard that God is with you. We will go with you.

The Jewish people are going to have a grand opportunity of salvation during the first three-and-a-half years of the Tribulation because of the ministry of the 144,000 Jewish evangelists described in Revelation 7:1-8 and 14:1-5.

> *And I heard the number of them which were sealed: and there were sealed an hundred and forty and four thousand of all the tribes of the children of Israel.* —REVELATION 7:4

> *...an hundred forty and four thousand, having his Father's name written in their foreheads.* —REVELATION 14:1

Right at the beginning of the seven-year Tribulation, God will choose 144,000 unmarried Jewish men, 12,000 out of each of the twelve Tribes of Israel. They are called servants of God — whose assignment is to get Israel saved. And while Israel is getting saved, ten Gentile men of other nations, races, tribes, and languages will be drawn to them, saying, "We've heard God's with you, we're going with you."

MULTITUDES, MULTITUDES IN THE VALLEY OF DECISION... (JOEL 3:14)

I read an article recently that said there are now approximately, sixteen million Jews in the world. I personally believe the number to be greater. Romans 11:26 does say, "All Israel shall be saved."

So you ask, "Do you believe that means every single individual one?"

Not necessarily. However, I do believe sufficient numbers of Jews from every tribe will be saved and fulfill the Scripture, allowing us to state that Israel was saved.

But let's hypothetically say that 12 million of them get saved, and also ten times that many Gentile men. That's another 120 million. Well when you get men, you're going to get women and children. Whatever the number will actually be, for every Jewish person that will be saved during the first half of the Tribulation period through the ministry of the 144,000 — there are going to be multitudes of Gentiles saved!

So, pre-raptured evangelism consists of the first phase of God's mercy. Then over the course of the first half of the Tribulation, the second phase of God's mercy will begin as the 144,000 unmarried Jewish men assume their responsibilities of preaching the Gospel. And the devil won't be able to stop them. Neither will Satan's Antichrist. These 144,000 Jewish servants of God will simply frustrate the daylights out of the Devil, the Antichrist, and his False Prophet.

All of Israel will be in the process of being saved along with masses of Gentiles during God's Phase-two mercy during the Tribulation. Together, this company will make up the great multitude that John describes in Revelation 7: 9-17:

> *After this I beheld, and, lo, a great multitude, which no man could number, of all nations, and kindreds, and people, and tongues, stood before the throne, and before the Lamb, clothed with white robes, and palms in their hands.... —* REVELATION 7:9

One of the elders asked John, **Who are they and from where do they come?** John turned to the elder and said, **Sir, you know.** So the elder answered His own question, **These are they which came out of great tribulation, and have washed their robes, and made them white in the blood of the Lamb** (v.14).

We see an additional rapture here in Revelation 7:9 that will occur at mid-Tribulation. I am persuaded to believe that company will number close to one billion people.

So God is merciful. By mid-Tribulation during the second phase of God's mercy all of Israel will be saved, except for a remnant. Then, those who have yet resisted will be hidden away for the second half of the Tribulation, as can be seen in Revelation 12:13,14.

And when the dragon saw that he was cast unto the earth, he persecuted the woman which brought forth the man child.

And to the woman were given two wings of a great eagle, that she might fly into the wilderness, into her place, where she is nourished for a time, and times, and half a time, from the face of the serpent. —REVELATION 12:13-14

God marvelously hides them away during the second half of the Tribulation, to prevent them from being destroyed by the Antichrist. And the Antichrist won't be able to find them.

Now if you're thinking, "Where in the world could people hide on the earth today, where they couldn't be found?"

Well I'll tell you, I don't know. But I do know that the Bible says the remnant of Israel will be hidden away for forty-two months. God will protect them over the period of 1,260 days that will make up the second half of the Tribulation. And I do believe the 144,000 will have to go with them into hiding, because it will be their responsibility to see to it that this remaining remnant gets saved. In the middle of the Great Tribulation, the public ministry of the 144,000 will end. Their remaining ministry will be exclusively private to the hidden remnant of Israel, which will introduce to the world God's third phase of mercy.

MERCY PHASE 3: THE GOSPEL VIA ANGELS

So who will the preach the Gospel after the 144,000 are gone? Angels. This is prophesied clearly in Revelation 14:6:

> *And I saw another angel fly in the midst of heaven, having the everlasting gospel to preach unto them that dwell on the earth, and to every nation, and kindred, and tongue, and people....*
> —REVELATION 14:6

When angels begin preaching the Gospel, the world will enter into the third phase of the mercy of God during the second half of the Great Tribulation.

STILL MORE MERCY FOR THE TRIBULATION SAINTS

What do you suppose would be happening by noon tomorrow in your home town if angels showed up at 10 o'clock in the morning and began preaching the Gospel to the entire area? This will be the reality of the second half of the Tribulation period.

Revelation 14:6 says angels will preach the everlasting Gospel.

Why?

Because God is merciful. He is so merciful that He doesn't want anyone to perish. He wants everyone to have an opportunity of salvation. So for the second half of the Tribulation period, angels will preach the Gospel. I firmly tell you, they're going to get results because the Word of God doesn't return void. (Isaiah 55:11.)

Revelation 14:6-9 further states this simple powerful Gospel mercifully warns people, "Do not take the mark of the beast."

MORE 666 PRE-TRIB NONSENSE

As I mentioned in chapter 2, there are many Christians today who are really disturbed over the mark of the beast. And the reason they are is because of what's being taught on Christian television. I'm sure these teachers mean well, and that, perhaps, they're sincere. But the manner in which they are presently teaching the mark of the beast, is wrong.

Why?

Because there is no mark of the beast today.

You say, "What?"

Again, I say, "There is no mark of the Beast today." The mark of the Beast appears on nothing today. Neither can it be received by anyone. When you study the Book of Revelation, you will discover there is perfect order of events in the book. Revelation chapter 13:16-18 reveals the mark of the Beast isn't introduced until the middle of the Tribulation. Not only that, you will find it isn't introduced by the Antichrist, but by the False Prophet. And by the middle of the Tribulation, the Church will have been in heaven for three-and-a-half years. We need to simply cease being fearful of the mark of the Beast!

So now point out, "But so many things seem to be headed in the direction of the Antichrist."

The information the television teachers have been pointing out only identifies some of the things the Antichrist may use once he comes on the scene. So pardon a little East Texas grammar but, "He ain't here yet." And he can't show up, as long as we're here. (See 2 Thessalonians 2:3,6-8.)

By way of review, the first phase of the mercy of God is taking place right now because of the sacrifice of Jesus and the preaching of the Gospel by the Church.

The second phase of the mercy of God will take place through the preaching of the Gospel by the 144,000 during the first half of the Tribulation.

And the third phase of the mercy of God will bless the world through the preaching of the Gospel by angels during the second half of the Tribulation — winning many converts! Which takes us now to the fourth and final phase of the mercy of God.

MERCY PHASE 4
SALVATION DURING THE MILLENNIUM

The fourth phase of the mercy of God will bless the earth during the thousand-year reign of Christ we know as the Millennium.

The Gospel will be preached during this thousand-year period, showing again God's eternal mercy. We know this because Revelation 21:23-25 makes a reference to nations that will be saved during that thousand-year period prior to the beginning of the new heaven, new earth, and new Jerusalem:

And the city had no need of the sun, neither of the moon, to shine in it: for the glory of God did lighten it, and the Lamb is the light thereof.

And the nations of them which are saved shall walk in the light of it: and the kings of the earth do bring their glory and honour into it.

And the gates of it shall not be shut at all by day: for there shall be no night there.

And they shall bring the glory and honour of the nations into it.

We are biblically aware of many unsaved people surviving the Tribulation due to the statement in Zechariah 14:16.

And it shall come to pass, that every one that is left of all the nations which came against Jerusalem shall even go up from year to year to worship the King, the LORD of hosts, and to keep the feast of tabernacles.

Therefore, unless they accept Jesus during His thousand-year reign, they can have no part in God's eternal plan, as is revealed in Revelation 21:27.

And there shall in no wise enter into it any thing that defileth, neither whatsoever worketh abomination, or maketh a lie: but they which are written in the Lamb's book of life.

We can also see that people will be saved during the Millennium in Isaiah's prophetic view of this rapidly approaching period in 66:19: **And I will set a sign among them, and I will send those that escape[2] of them unto the nations, to Tarshish, Pul, and Lud, that draw the bow, to Tubal, and Javan, to the isles afar off, that have not heard my fame, neither have seen my glory....**

What will "those" Isaiah writes of, escape?

---

[2] Strong's James. " Hebrew and Chaldee Dictionary of the Old Testament, *Strong's Exhaustive Concordance of the Bible*, Nashville: Abingdon, 1890, p. 95 # 6412.

The Tribulation period. The Tribulation will be the period immediately precedent to the thousand-year reign of Christ. As you will notice in my footnote, the Hebrew word for escape also means, *refugee*.

And what will those do who have escaped?

...and they shall declare my glory among the Gentiles. And they shall bring all your brethren for an offering unto the Lord out of all nations.

"They" will declare the glory of God among the nations and bring an offering to the Lord.

And in litters, and upon mules, and upon swift beasts, to my holy mountain Jerusalem, saith the Lord, as the children of Israel bring an offering in a clean vessel into the house of the Lord. And I will also take of them for priests and for Levites, saith the Lord. Of course, in Isaiah's day, horses and chariots were the best vehicles.

Those who have escaped (survived) this seven-year period, are those who will be saved during the second half of the Tribulation; through angelic ministry.

Now follow me...Revelation 7:9 indicates that those who are saved during the first half of the Tribulation will be raptured mid-Tribulation.] But those who get saved during the second half of the Tribulation, will not be raptured. Who is also saved during the second half of the Tribulation? The remnant of Israel who will be preached to by the 144,000 during their time of hiding, and those who will be saved through the preaching of angels prophesied in Revelation 14.

So I am confident this prophecy of Isaiah tells us that those who will be saved out of the second half of the Great Tribulation will be "those" of chapter 66 of His book. They will be "those" who will declare God's glory and fame to the nations to bring them as an offering to Him during the thousand-year reign of Christ.

Without question, those who are raptured before and during the first half of the Tribulation will be serving in special assignments. This passage of Isaiah shows us, however, that the major soulwinning assignments will rest with the converts of the second half of the Tribulation.

The mercy of God continues to be extended, as it is not God's will that any should perish, but that all should come to repentance.

God's mercy will even curtail the processes of death during the thousand-year reign of Christ. Death won't be operating then as it does today. The prophet Isaiah says if a man during that period were to die at one hundred years old, he would still be considered a child. (Isaiah 65:20.) So longevity of life will be wonderfully restored.

The mercy of God will also remove the horrors of war during the Millennium's coming thousand years. (Isaiah 2:4; Micah 4:3.) And the mercy of God will forbid he who has the power of death, the devil, during that period, imprisoning him in the bottomless pit. (Revelation 20:1-3.)

But as marvelous as it would be for everyone to get saved during the Millennium, we know from the book of Revelation that this won't happen. Satan will be released at the end of the thousand-year reign of Christ for just a short season. And when he is, he will gather those others that Revelation 21:27 says will be forbidden to enter the New Jerusalem. Other rebels who resisted God's mercy during this merciful time period will move against the city of Jerusalem with their deceiver, Satan. When they do, they will be met with God's supernatural fire that will consume his followers.

After this Satan will be cast into the lake of fire to join his False Prophet and the Antichrist.

Then the wicked will be resurrected to be judged at the Great White Throne of Judgment to receive their place of eternal punishment.

> *Blessed are the merciful: for they shall obtain mercy.* —MATTHEW 5:7

So then, when we understand the everlasting power of God's kindness and mercy that will truly endure forever, we should be ever more merciful in the here and now. We should be moved to preach the Gospel of Jesus Christ's mercy while our time is at hand, so fewer will have to face the Tribulation's scourge. We should be lending ourselves to sharpen the barbs of God's fence that surrounds the gates of hell through our bold proclamation of the Gospel of Jesus' shed blood, the power of the Holy Spirit, and the power of Jesus' name.

So let's not cut anyone off. Regardless of how wicked, violent, contemptible, immoral, godless, or like Satan they may be. Let's show them God's mercy. Let's believe God for their salvation. It is not God's will that any should perish, but that all should come to repentance. Thank God for His mercy. Thank God that we live in a kingdom of mercy!

CHAPTER 9

THE SEASON OF THE RAPTURE

CHAPTER NINE

THE SEASON OF THE RAPTURE

But of that day and that hour knoweth no man, no not the angels which are in heaven, neither the Son, but the Father. Take ye heed, watch and pray; for ye know not when the time is.
—MARK 13:32-33

As the seasons of Church history have come and gone, the appearing of Jesus has been anticipated in each of them. And though there has never been one as near to the event as ours, Jesus was emphatic that NO ONE, except our Heavenly Father, would know the time of His appearing to receive the Church. To be ready and expecting at a moment's notice is the only directive Christ gave the Church.

Everyone who studies the Scriptures knows that Jesus will return one day to reign on earth for a thousand years, but that wasn't what He was talking about in the

141

above cited verse out of Mark 13, as many assume. The day of His return will occur on the last day of a seven year fixed timeframe of the Tribulation. And the Tribulation will occur over the last seven exact years before Christ's millennial reign as prophesied by both Daniel and John.

Both Daniel and John's time frames equate to 84 months or 2,520 days. And both of these prophets divide the seven years of tribulation into two equal halves of 3 1/2 years, or 42 months, or 1260 days. Several other events also have a fixed time within the Tribulation's timeframe, such as the ministry of the two witnesses in Jerusalem, recorded Revelation 11, and the movement of a huge 200 million man army described in Revelation 9. In fact, the seasons of these prophetic activities are so exact, that should one have failed to begin a countdown of the Tribulation's seven years at its beginning, these fixed times would allow an accurate countdown to the day Christ Jesus returns to planet earth.

Therefore the day in which Jesus will appear in the air, to catch away the Church, cannot be determined.

Why?

Because Jesus said no one, not even Himself or the angels in heaven, except the Father would know the day or hour of that blessed expectant event. Jesus did, however, give us a command to be ready and expectant. That's why He said in Mark 13:33, **Take ye heed, watch and pray; for ye know not when the time is.**

So please pay close attention to the next four verses:

For the Son of man is as a man taking a far journey, who left his house, and gave authority to his servants, and to every man his work, and commanded the porter to watch.

Watch ye therefore: for ye know not when the master of the house cometh, at even, or at midnight, or at the cockcrowing, or in the morning:

Lest coming suddenly he find you sleeping.

And what I say unto you I say unto all, Watch. —MARK 13:34-37

Jesus provided an excellent illustration within these verses that strongly exhorts His followers to stay spiritually aware and ready to go at a moment's notice right up to the actual time of His appearance, described in Matthew 24:44:

Therefore be ye also ready: for in such an hour as ye think not the Son of man cometh (v.44).

SO JESUS ALSO CONTINUED HERE:

> *Who then is a faithful and wise servant, whom
> his lord hath made ruler over his household, to
> give them meat in due season?*
>
> *Blessed is that servant, whom his lord when
> he cometh shall find so doing.* —MATTHEW 24:45,46

I can't say enough: It is of utmost importance that
the followers of Jesus remain true to Him and maintain
their intimate salvation relationship.

And keep in mind that if Jesus knew the day and
hour of the catching away of the Church, He would tell
us. Because in John 15:15 He said, **But I have called
you friends, for all things that I have heard of my
Father I have made known unto you.**

But we can know the season in which this very
important event will occur.

The season in which Jesus is to appear was clearly
established through several of His own prophecies and
other Old Testament prophets. In Luke 21:24-36, Jesus
detailed a time in which the Gentile control of Jerusalem
will end along with a series of prophesied events.

And they shall fall by the edge of the sword, and shall be led away captive into all nations: and Jerusalem shall be trodden down of the Gentiles, until the times of the Gentiles be fulfilled.

And there shall be signs in the sun, and in the moon, and in the stars; and upon the earth distress of nations, with perplexity; the sea and the waves roaring;

Men's hearts failing them for fear, and for looking after those things which are coming on the earth: for the powers of heaven shall be shaken.

And then shall they see the Son of man coming in a cloud with power and great glory.

And when these things begin to come to pass, then look up, and lift up your heads; for your redemption draweth nigh.

And he spake to them a parable; Behold the fig tree, and all the trees;

When they now shoot forth, ye see and know of your own selves that summer is now nigh at hand.

So likewise ye, when ye see these things come to pass, know ye that the kingdom of God is nigh at hand.

145

Verily I say unto you, This generation shall not pass away, till all be fulfilled.

Heaven and earth shall pass away: but my words shall not pass away.

And take heed to yourselves, lest at any time your hearts be overcharged with surfeiting, and drunkenness, and cares of this life, and so that day come upon you unawares.

For as a snare shall it come on all them that dwell on the face of the whole earth.

Watch ye therefore, and pray always, that ye may be accounted worthy to escape all these things that shall come to pass, and to stand before the Son of man. —LUKE 21:24-36

Gentile occupation of the ancient city of Jerusalem began with Babylonian control almost six hundred years before the birth of Jesus, then ended during the Six-day War in June of 1967.

But Gentile domination of Jerusalem will once again take place during the second half of the Tribulation when the Antichrist moves from Europe to Jerusalem according to 2 Thessalonians 2:4 and Revelation 11:2. At that time, the final phase of the abomination of the holy place prophesied by Daniel and Jesus will have been fulfilled.

SIGNS IN THE SUN, MOON AND STARS

Jesus continues in verse 25 describing signs in the sun, moon and stars, during a time in which all nations will be experiencing internal distress caused by the roaring of the sea.

An examination of scientific records in the field of astronomy proves that the sun, moon and stars have never deviated from their patterns of operation originally established by God. But they will when the season is right for the fulfillment of God's events.

The activities of man's space exploration could also account for some signs in the heavens.

It was in 1968, one year after Israel repossessed the city of Jerusalem, that America's astronauts were launched in a Saturn 5 missile from Cape Kennedy, Florida, toward the moon. Two hundred and forty thousand miles later they went into a sixty hinc orbit of the planet moon as space suddenly became a celestial observation platform of God's front yard — and the world received its first live TV pictures of our earth from moon.

147

Since 1968, we have sent up space vehicles examining every other major planet in our galaxy. Most recently in 1990, NASA launched the Hubble Space Telescope. And if there has ever been a testimony to the reality and glory of mankind and God the Creator of heaven and earth, it has certainly been evident in these satellite routed signs beamed back from the heavens that declare His glory.

During the years of 1969 through 1971, we traveled with our astronauts by television as they walked and drove on the moon and as many of them found God through the experience because of the sign of God's handiwork in outer space.

But at the same time that our space program was accomplishing these events never achieved by man, earth's nations below were exploding in ethnic riots, chaos, demonstrations, civil unrest, and upheavals of epic proportions.

The "seas" are currently roaring with national strife around the world. Seas, according to the Beast's symbolism in Revelation 13:1 are people. So the roaring of the sea in Jesus' prophecy in Matthew 24:7 is nothing more than masses of people, nation against nation, or as the Greek sets forth *ethnos* against *ethnos* — one race against another — in a state of intense unrest.[1]

As the years of space exploration and massive unrest continued to develop, the number one killer on earth became *FEAR*. Luke 21:26 confirms this fact. And we must realize that the upheaval of nations caused by difficult internal problems will continue until the day Christ and His Church return from heaven to earth. Stress caused by fear of the unknown will continue to cause multiple deaths by heart failure.

Now here is the key seasonal verse spoken by Jesus in verse 28 of Luke 21:

> *And when these things **begin** to come to pass, then look up, and lift up your heads; for your redemption draweth nigh.*

In this prophetic statement Jesus pointed out that we are to look for the final act of redemption when these prophecies *begin* to be fulfilled, not when they are fulfilled. The final act of redemption will take place at

---

[1] Strong, James. "Greek Dictionary of the New Testament," *Strong's Exhaustive Concordance of the Bible,* Nashville: Abingdon, 1890, p. 25, #1484.

Christ's appearing when the redeemed will receive the glorification of their bodies. Paul tells us in 1 Corinthians 15:51-53 that this changing event will take place in the "twinkling of an eye."

The word "look"[2] used in Luke 21:28 by Jesus, means to *eagerly anticipate the event with joyous preparation.*

Then, to help those of us anticipating and "looking" for the season of His blessed appearing, Jesus gave us the clues of His season through the story of the fig tree in Luke 21:29-36.

> *And he spake to them a parable; Behold the fig tree, and all the trees;*
>
> *When they now shoot forth, ye see and know of your own selves that summer is now nigh at hand.*
>
> *So likewise ye, when ye see these things come to pass, know ye that the kingdom of God is nigh at hand.*
>
> *Verily I say unto you, This generation shall not pass away, till all be fulfilled.*

---

[2] Strong, James. "Greek Dictionary of the New Testament," *Strong's Exhaustive Concordance of the Bible,* Nashville: Abingdon, 1890, p.11, # 352.

Heaven and earth shall pass away: but my words shall not pass away.

And take heed to yourselves, lest at any time your hearts be overcharged with surfeiting, and drunkenness, and cares of this life, and so that day come upon you unawares.

For as a snare shall it come on all them that dwell on the face of the whole earth.

Watch ye therefore, and pray always, that ye may be accounted worthy to escape all those things that shall come to pass, and to stand before the Son of man. —LUKE 21:29-36

The Church has been instructed throughout my lifetime by ministers and theologians that the fig tree in this passage is symbolic of Israel. And such teachings prove to be correct based on Jeremiah chapter 24, along with other references.

Therefore, since the fig tree is a type of Israel, all the other trees in Christ's statement must relate to other nations. Because to be consistent with biblical interpretation, we must understand that Jesus would never change directions in the middle of a verse.

...THE FIG TREE AND *ALL* THE TREES...

Today, more than forty nations are actively involved in the fulfillment of the Scriptures. First of all, the United States, without question, is the number one supporter of Israel and is very actively involved. At the same time, we have faced the very difficult task of consistently making the Arab world know that we aren't their enemy. This sensitive diplomacy has been handled well by our state department, being the only diplomatic corps in the world capable of handling the complications of the Middle East.

Along with US support, the European economic community (common market nations) also support Israel. In fact, Israel is an associate member of the common market.

Arab nations of the world are also participating in bringing about the fulfillment of the last day's prophecies. Without exception they declared war on Israel May 15, 1918. Their declaration and subsequent actions without doubt began to fulfill the Day of the Lord prophesied in Zephaniah 2:1.

> *Gather yourselves together, yea, gather together, O nation not desired....*

As of this writing Egypt and Jordan have made peace with Israel. And the others will follow in due time because peace in that region is clearly prophesied in Ezekiel 38:8,11,14-15.

The Orient is also currently playing a key prophetic role. The industrialization of many Oriental and southeast Asian countries, which has removed them from the list of third world countries, is presently providing a source for the 200,000,000 man army prophesied in Revelation chapter 9. This army will advance overland during the last thirteen months of the Tribulation then join with the armies of the Antichrist for the Battle of Armageddon.

LOOK OUT FOR GOG

But clearly, one of the most visual nations in the prophetic picture today is Russia. She is identified as Gog from the land of Magog, Meshech and Tubal in Ezekiel 38, verses 2 and 3.

Son of man, set thy face against Gog, the land of Magog, the chief prince of Meshech and Tubal, and prophesy against him,

And say, Thus saith the Lord GOD; Behold, I am against thee, O Gog, the chief prince of Meshech and Tubal....

In this outstanding prophetic chapter it is clear that Russia, from the far north, intends to one day invade and control Israel.

Gog's action will bring about World War III at the onset of the Tribulation in which God will step in to defend Israel through the use of His wrath, necessitating the catching away of the Church prior to the use of His wrath. (See Ezekiel 38:19; 1 Thessalonians 1:10; and 1 Thessalonians 5:9-10.)

WHY RAPTURE — BEFORE WRATH?

There are some who ask "why?" the Church must be removed before earth's judgment by God's wrath. The answer is simple. An overview of the Holy Scriptures reveals that God's established pattern of operation is to always remove the righteous ones prior to the use of *His* wrath. Keep in mind, God and His ways are perfect. So once He establishes a pattern of operation He will never change it, because it was perfect to begin with.

For example, in Genesis 6 and 7, God told Noah of the coming flood. Second Peter 2:5 reveals that through Noah's righteous preaching, God provided ample warning for the people. Genesis reveals how God instructed Noah to build an ark for the saving of his righteous household. The ark is a type of the Rapture of the Church.

When it came time for the flood, God ordered Noah and his family into the animal-laden ark and closed its door. Then when the flood (God's wrath,) came, Noah and his family were above God's wrath, (in the ark.) The righteous were spared the flood, being brought to safety above it until God's wrath subsided, and the ark brought them back to earth.

You will also find this and other examples in my book, *The Rapture, Get Right or Get Left.* I highly recommend that you get a copy of this book and study it thoroughly with the Scriptures to more fully understand God's unchangeable, perfect ways. They all reveal an exact duplicate pattern of the catching away of the Church.

Once the Church is caught away, we will remain above the wrath of God on earth, like Noah, until the wrath ends. At that time, the Church will return to earth with Jesus for a thousand years.

The pattern is divinely set and cannot be changed. The most distinct Scriptures revealing this truth are found in 1 Thessalonians 1:10 where Paul says:

*And to wait for his Son from heaven, whom he raised from the dead, even Jesus, **which delivered us from the wrath to come.***

Then in chapter 5: 9,10 he says:

For God hath not appointed us to wrath, but to obtain salvation by our Lord Jesus Christ, Who died for us, that, whether we wake or sleep, we should live together with him.

Therefore, when the fig tree and all the other trees have been fully considered, and we are ready and looking up as our redemption draws near, we can be comforted in knowing that the season of His appearing is the season of our escape. And those signs are all upon us presently, so look up, stay awake!

THE SEASON OF THE ANTICHRIST AND HIS BEAST SYSTEM

THE SEASON OF THE ANTICHRIST AND HIS BEAST SYSTEM

No one you know on earth needs to be on earth after the Church is raptured and the Tribulation begins. Because in the course of time, when the season is ripe for his own evil appearing, a world ruler will arise on the earth whose sole purpose will be to destroy anyone who opposes Satan's will. He will do this through the establishment of a governmental system which is spoken of in great detail, in the Book of Revelation.

Revelation 13 provides detailed insight into the meaning of this coming Beast's system through his picture of seven crowned heads and ten horns. His prophetic description is an exact likeness of the dragon's picture introduced by Revelation 12:3. So Satan will be the direct source and provide the authority of the Beast and his system because it will be like him. The Beast is Bible prophecy's infamous Antichrist.

THE SYSTEM

In the following vivid description, John uses the name blasphemy to further identify the Beast with Satan:

And I stood upon the sand of the sea, and saw a beast rise up out of the sea, having seven heads and ten horns, and upon his horns ten crowns, and upon his heads the name of blasphemy. —REVELATION 13:1

The Beast system will be the product of Satan's work through people. The sea out of which it will come will not be a body of water, but masses of people — the sea of humanity. Just as God accomplishes His plan through human agents, so does Satan.

THE BEAST'S FATAL WOUND

And I saw one of his heads as it were wounded to death; and his deadly wound was healed: and all the world wondered after the beast (v.3).

Some teachers declare that the man who will head the Beast System, the Antichrist, will be assassinated, then resurrected by the False Prophet to deceive the whole world. But such teaching is unsound and inharmonious with the entire biblical story.

Why?

As I have pointed out in a number of my other books, it would be impossible for the False Prophet to resurrect the Antichrist. Because only God the Holy Ghost has resurrection power, and He would not resurrect this ungodly man.

One of the Beast's heads in John's vision is shown to be wounded unto death. And each head represents a kingdom. So, as I pointed out in chapter 6, because the seal of Daniel 12 has been lifted, we know from studying the biblical and historical records that the Beast's fatal wound represents the destruction of one of the world great empires, the Roman Empire.

When a symbolic vision is to be interpreted in Bible prophecy, a literal symbolic interpretation is usually in order. King Nebuchadnezzar had a dream in Daniel chapter 2 that revealed the coming kingdoms of the world that would be eventually destroyed by the first coming of Christ:

> *And in the days of these kings shall the God of heaven set up a kingdom, which shall never be destroyed: and the kingdom shall not be left to other people, but it shall break in pieces and consume all these kingdoms, and it shall stand for ever.* —DANIEL 2:44

Then Nebuchadnezzer saw a stone, which fell on every kingdom, which was revealed to be the kingdom of God:

> *Forasmuch as thou sawest that the stone was cut out of the mountain without hands, and that it brake in pieces the iron, the brass, the clay, the silver, and the gold; the great God hath made known to the king what shall come to pass hereafter: and the dream is certain, and the interpretation thereof sure* (v. 45).

The stone destroyed the great image that was earlier interpreted to represent the Babylonian, Persian, Greek, and Roman Empires, and represented the first coming of Jesus. So when the Church Age began, Jesus wounded the sixth head to death.

The fall of the Roman Empire caused the demise of the entire system, which will indeed be resurrected by Satan, amazing all the world.

Preceding his statement concerning the wounded head (v. 3), John is still supplying information about the total system he calls the Beast. The man who eventually heads the system is also called a beast. Remember to differentiate between the two. It is the system and not the man who is mortally wounded.

Now in verse 5, John begins referring to the man who will have authority and head the vast system.

THE ANTICHRIST

And they worshipped the dragon which gave power unto the beast: and they worshipped the beast, saying, Who is like unto the beast? who is able to make war with him?

And there was given unto him a mouth speaking great things and blasphemies; and power was given unto him to continue forty and two months. —REVELATION 13:4,5

The Beast System will be given a voice that speaks great things and blasphemies. He will be given authority to continue for forty-two months. As is generally known, the season of this man who will become the Antichrist will not ripen and take this image upon himself until the last half of the Tribulation. During the first half he will attempt to pass himself off as a man of peace.

In his season, this coming deceiver will be an outstanding leader of the European states, a diplomat of the first order. Using his ability to combine the governments, commerce, military and religion of the ten nations, he will personally affect the resurrection of the Beast System.

He will also be successful in establishing himself as the head of his coming system. Then at mid-Tribulation he will begin his attempt to conquer the world. In chapter 9 of his book, Daniel prophesied the Antichrist's breaking of the agreement he will have made with Israel, that will propel him into his pursuits of becoming world dictator.

> *And he shall confirm the covenant with many for one week: and in the midst of the week he shall cause the sacrifice and the oblation to cease, and for the overspreading of abominations he shall make it desolate, even until the consummation, and that determined shall be poured upon the desolate.* —DANIEL 9:27

> *And he opened his mouth in blasphemy against God, to blaspheme his name, and his tabernacle, and them that dwell in heaven.* —REVELATION 13:6

The Antichrist will blaspheme the many people who have escaped him and his system, but to no avail. They will be in heaven!

> *And it was given unto him to make war with the saints, and to overcome them: and power was given him over all kindreds, and tongues, and nations* (v.7).

The Church company will already stand before the throne of God when this scene takes place. The saints referred to in the above verse are not the believers of the Church Age but the saints of the Tribulation, the converts of the 144,000 Jewish evangelists.

Verse 7 states that the Antichrist will be given power over all kindreds, languages and nations at the height of his season.

Verse 2 reveals that Satan will give him that authority. He will have satanic authority and power to make war against and overcome the 144,000, their converts and the hidden remnant of Israel, but he will find this impossible. Remember, Satan has used numerous other men through the centuries in his attempt to crush the Church and gain control over the world. But Satan's power and authority don't begin to compare with

God's. If the Antichrist's assignment in his coming season were actually from God, he would succeed. However, it will come from Satan, and will therefore fail despite the tremendous vehicles he will utilize.

After the Antichrist breaks his agreement with Israel at mid-Tribulation, he will attempt to make war with her people. But he will fail because the converts of the 144,000 will have either been hidden away or caught up into heaven.[1]

And all that dwell upon the earth shall worship him, whose names are not written in the book of life of the Lamb slain from the foundation of the world.

If any man have an ear, let him hear.

He that leadeth into captivity shall go into captivity: he that killeth with the sword must be killed with the sword. Here is the patience and the faith of the saints (vv.8-10).

As I have pointed out, all who dwell on the earth will not include the 144,000 Jewish evangelists, the remnant of Israel, the Arabs who resist the Antichrist (Zechariah

---

[1] Revelation 7:9;12:14;14:1-5.

14; Isaiah 19) and many Gentiles (Zechariah 8:23). God will command their attention. The Chinese and their million man army (Revelation 9:16) will run a direct collision course with the Antichrist's plans, and according to Daniel 11:44, cause him trouble.

But tidings out of the east and out of the north shall trouble him: therefore he shall go forth with great fury to destroy, and utterly to make away many.

The statement, **If anyone has an ear, let him hear,** clearly reveals that God will be attempting to gain the attention of all people during this time. He will be saying in this coming season of darkness and intrigue, "If you listen to and obey Me, you won't be caught in this satanic system."

But isn't that what God is saying through His Church today? Have you been saying it to keep those you know out of the Tribulation's day? No one you know needs to experience the Antichrist's season. So stay steady and keep preaching. Those who don't have ears to hear today, may tomorrow.

CHAPTER 11

THE SEASON OF
THE FALSE PROPHET
AND THE MARK OF THE BEAST

THE SEASON OF
THE FALSE PROPHET
AND THE MARK OF THE BEAST

The Antichrist will have in his coming season a
human accomplice shrouded in the deception of his own
satanic calling, who will be given the assignment of
deceiving the nations religiously. He will look like a lamb
(a legitimate spiritual leader). But he will speak like a
dragon (Satan himself), and he will work to draw the
world's worship to the image of the beast.

*And I beheld another beast coming up out of
the earth; and he had two horns like a lamb, and
he spake as a dragon.*

*And he exerciseth all the power of the first
beast before him, and causeth the earth and them
which dwell therein to worship the first beast,
whose deadly wound was healed.*

And he doeth great wonders, so that he maketh fire come down from heaven on the earth in the sight of men,

And deceiveth them that dwell on the earth, by the means of those miracles which he had power to do in the sight of the beast; saying to them that dwell on the earth, that they should make an image to the beast, which had the wound by a sword, and did live.

And he had power to give life unto the image of the beast, that the image of the beast should both speak, and cause that as many as would not worship the image of the beast should be killed.
—REVELATION 13:11-15

In the evil season of his appearing, the False Prophet will bring with his appointment great deception, causing many people on the earth to worship the Antichrist and his system. To do this, he will have cunning occult powers.

Of the Antichrist's operation, Paul says there will be lying wonders (2 Thessalonians 2:9). These will be clever maneuvers designed to appear as genuine miracles in an attempt to deceive all mankind. But none of the works of either the Antichrist or the False Prophet will be true miracles.

The False Prophet will create an image of the Beast then threaten to kill all who won't worship it. The image will have apparent cultic powers to communicate. Keep in mind that the Beast System will not be worldwide and will be operating from its European base. Worship of the image will introduce idolatry, which God has always rejected. (Leviticus 26:1.)

THE MARK OF THE BEAST

As I have mentioned in previous chapters, there has been great controversy and speculation concerning the exact design of the Beast's coming mark. And too many Christians are fruitlessly concerned today about its current effect on them. It won't even become an issue until it is initiated by the False Prophet in this chapter of Revelation during the Antichrist's season. And by then, the Church will be in heaven, raptured, gone:

And he causeth all, both small and great, rich and poor, free and bond, to receive a mark in their right hand, or in their foreheads:

And that no man might buy or sell, save he that had the mark, or the name of the beast, or the number of his name.

173

Here is wisdom. Let him that hath understanding count the number of the beast: for it is the number of a man; and his number is Six hundred threescore and six (vv.16-18).

The most outstanding characteristic of the beast's infamous mark will be its association with the number 666. We shouldn't speculate about its design beyond this, because the Scripture isn't specific.

Some of the more fruitless speculations of the mark's supposed current presence alarm people when a phone number, street address or license plate contains the number 666. Someone has pointed out that the license number on many of the commercial vehicles in Israel begins with an ominous 666.[1] This is superstition! The number 666 itself is not significant. It will only be significant when it actually identifies those people who become part of the Beast System during the second half of the Tribulation period.

As I have also pointed out, this is not to say that there aren't a number of forerunners of the Beast's mark

---

[1] Many commercial vehicles owned by Arabs in Israel have license plate numbers beginning with 666. Through this method, the Israelis can quickly identify the Arabs in case of emergency.

system already in place today. For the sake of speed and efficiency, every major concern identifies its customers by an account number. But our current accounting systems aren't satanic. Neither is our use of credit cards, or the Social Security as some have alarmed. These systems are only forerunners of the Antichrist's attempts to take over world commerce.

The Antichrist and his False Prophet will have a period of exactly seven years to carry out their plan of world conquest. At mid-Tribulation, they will take over European governments. Then they will move to take over the religious systems by calling for the Beast's worship, which is idolatry, then world commerce by the issuance of the identification mark.

666
THE DEADLY NUMBER THAT WILL ULTIMATELY FAIL

According to biblical numerology, a man's number is six. It indicates "incompleteness." The number of the Beast System is three sixes. Therefore, his system will be an incomplete operation which will fail. Since the entire structure will be designed by the dragon (Satan), it will be very destructive in its season of operation, but imperfect. Apply the three sixes to the three imperfect beings that will attempt to rule the world through the Beast system, and we can visualize an evil trinity: Satan, the Antichrist and the False Prophet.

As the Tribulation progresses, the situation on earth will become increasingly more critical, especially during the last half in the geographical areas held by the Beast System. There will be less commercial operation, because there will be very little left to buy or sell due to famine and wars. Through the mark of the Beast, the Antichrist will attempt to take over as much of the world's remaining commercial operation as possible.

To continue buying and selling, one will have to take the mark of the system's identification on either the right hand or the forehead. The system will use the mark and the threat of death to coerce people to surrender. As I showed previously through the words of the angel's simple gospel during the second half of the Tribulation, if anyone takes the mark or worships the Beast's image, it will seal their doom. There will be no possibility of salvation for them:

> *And the third angel followed them, saying with a loud voice, If any man worship the beast*

and his image, and receive his mark in his forehead, or in his hand,

The same shall drink of the wine of the wrath of God, which is poured out without mixture into the cup of his indignation; and he shall be tormented with fire and brimstone in the presence of the holy angels, and in the presence of the Lamb:

And the smoke of their torment ascendeth up for ever and ever: and they have no rest day nor night, who worship the beast and his image, and whosoever receiveth the mark of his name.[2] —
REVELATION 14:9-11

When his season is ready for harvest, the Beast and his prophet will move into the Jerusalem temple to exalt himself above all that is called God, as Paul writes in 2 Thessalonians 2:

Let no man deceive you by any means: for that day shall not come, except there come a falling away first, and that man of sin be revealed, the son of perdition;

---

[2] This is supernatural opposition to the receiving of the mark of the Beast — carried out by godly angels.

*Who opposeth and exalteth himself above all
that is called God, or that is worshipped; so that
he as God sitteth in the temple of God, shewing
himself that he is God.* —2 THESSALONIANS 2:3-4

But He and his False Prophet will have a major
problem: The strands of God's barbed wire fence around
hell will still be in place, and God's mercy will continually hamper their way. Every one of the vial judgments
unleashed in Revelation chapter 16 will destroy the
Beast's system and its marked people once it is barely
under way.

CHAPTER 12

THE SEASON OF THE HARLOT

THE SEASON OF THE HARLOT

We have already examined the onslaught of false worship and deception the Antichrist and his False Prophet will introduce during the Tribulation period. They "will" introduce it in the future tense because their season is not yet here. But the Book of Revelation also reveals another satanic cult system which started centuries ago that will play into the Antichrist's hands: Mystery Babylon, the harlot, who will personify every false religion that has appeared since mankind's fall. She will be the amalgamation of all man's religions into one organization and will move to deceive millions with her false powers.

False religion has plagued this planet since true faith was introduced. Undertake a brief historical study of the Mesopotamian plain on which the garden of Eden was located and you will discover the incredible onslaught of idolatry Satan immediately introduced after Adam and Eve's fall. It has flourished in the East for six millenniums, and most recently flooded into the West during America's rebellious '60s.

So the most important aspect of this chapter on the mystery cult harlot, is that her season has been...and is currently...here.

Paul wrote of her followers in 1 Timothy 4:1-3:

Now the Spirit speaketh expressly, that in the latter times some shall depart from the faith, giving heed to seducing spirits, and doctrines of devils;

Speaking lies in hypocrisy; having their conscience seared with a hot iron;

Forbidding to marry, and commanding to abstain from meats, which God hath created to be received with thanksgiving of them which believe and know the truth.

Today, we can clearly see her deceptive fruit in bloom as millions are being deceived through her seductive religious will. The aggressive assault of the Hindu Upanishad in the West brought into America the drugs and idolatry of Hinduism which subsequently spun off the myriad's of new age religions popular in the West today. Anywhere you find Yoga practiced, you will find an open door to the harlot's Hindu idolatry.

You will also see the harlot's fruit blooming on America's new psychic TV programs. These broadcasts were unheard of just a few years ago. But today, the harlot's message of godless "inner-peace" is aired coast-to-coast as viewers are invited to have their fortunes told over expensive psychic hotlines.

So, the harlot is certainly on the move.

In the fullness of her season, the harlot will once again move to dominate the world as was common in antiquity. But she will falter and ultimately be destroyed during her height in the Tribulation:

> *And there came one of the seven angels which had the seven vials, and talked with me, saying unto me, Come hither; I will shew unto thee the judgment of the great whore that sitteth upon many waters:*
>
> *With whom the kings of the earth have committed fornication, and the inhabitants of the earth have been made drunk with the wine of her fornication.*

So he carried me away in the spirit into the wilderness: and I saw a woman sit upon a scarlet colored beast, full of names of blasphemy, having seven heads and ten horns.

And the woman was arrayed in purple and scarlet color, and decked with gold and precious stones and pearls, having a golden cup in her hand full of abominations and filthiness of her fornication:

And upon her forehead was a name written, MYSTERY, BABYLON THE GREAT, THE MOTHER OF HARLOTS AND ABOMINATIONS OF THE EARTH.

And I saw the woman drunken with the blood of the saints, and with the blood of the martyrs of Jesus: and when I saw her, I wondered with great admiration. —REVELATION 17:1-6

The waters of verse 1 are peoples, nations, races and languages. (v. 15.) This great harlot (whore) in the season of her appearing will have had such vast influence over masses of people that she will be in control over entire nations. The kings of the earth will have committed fornication with her, and the inhabitants of the earth will be drunk with the wine of her fornication. What a horrible scene!

Fornication (v.2) refers to false religion, which has a form of godliness but denies the power thereof. (2 Timothy 3:5.) It substitutes religious rights and membership for true repentance and salvation. God considers all people who worship anyone or anything besides Himself participants in spiritual fornication and adultery.

In Revelation 17 she is pictured riding the Antichrist's seven headed beast, as a symbol of her influence in the last days. The heads in their season will be great kingdoms the two horns, lesser kingdoms, much of which will be looked at in great detail in this chapter. Because the harlot of Revelation has been supported by the Beast System since its beginning.

This woman John viewed was arrayed in purple and scarlet, and adorned with gold and precious stones and pearls, having in her hand a golden cup full of abominations and the filthiness of her fornication. And on her forehead a name was written: MYSTERY, BABYLON THE GREAT, THE MOTHER OF HARLOTS AND ABOMINATIONS OF THE EARTH (vv. 4,5).

In this description and list of names, MYSTERY is the first name that identifies the harlot. She will be of the utmost religious nature — mystical, spiritualistic. History bears out the fact that she dominated the seven great empires represented by the heads she is pictured riding in Revelation 17. As I pointed out in opening this chapter, the archaeology of the Sumarian plain has proven a myriad of false wooden and stone gods that this mystery sorceress has overseen. So it is not surprising to note that spiritualist mediums or people who practiced witchcraft controlled the leaders of the great empires from the time of Egypt until the fall of the Roman Empire.

The harlot's second title is BABYLON THE GREAT, which identifies her religious system with ancient Babylon, and clearly shows her influence over every successive Gentile empire.

The harlot's third title, THE MOTHER OF HARLOTS, indicates that every evil and destructive thing on earth will result from Satan's operation through her.

Her fourth title, THE MOTHER OF...ABOMINATIONS OF THE EARTH, reveals her total rejection by God.

HER SEASON OF OPERATION

The harlot has operated over a vast period of time. The Gentile empires resulted from Israel's collapse and captivity. History records that with the Assyrian Empire the system was ushered in. The Egyptian Empire, the first head of the Beast System, enslaved the family of Israel. When God delivered them, they established the great nation of Israel. Then came their rebellion and captivity. Assyria was the Gentile empire which initiated Israel's captivity by taking the ten northern tribes. The southern tribes of Judah were taken into Babylonian captivity about 107 years later. Nebuchadnezzar's dream in Daniel chapter 2 (spoken of in chapter 9) begins with the Babylonian Empire after Israel's total captivity

With the fall of the Roman Empire, the entire system crumbled. The harlot, which had a controlling influence on Gentile empires, was responsible for the death of many of God's saints, including those of the Early Church. In Revelation 17, as in chapter 12, John is tying historical records to future events.

THE SEVEN KINGDOMS

Though briefly covered when discussing the Antichrist's picture (Revelation 13) and Nebuchadnezzar's dream in Daniel, chapter 2, it is the harlot's prophetic picture in Revelation 17 that specifically points out the significance of each of the head's representation of a kingdom of the past.

And here is the mind which hath wisdom. The seven heads are seven mountains, on which the woman sitteth.

And there are seven kings: five are fallen, and one is, and the other is not yet come; and when he cometh, he must continue a short space.

And the beast that was, and is not, even he is the eighth, and is of the seven, and goeth into perdition.

And the ten horns which thou sawest are ten kings, which have received no kingdom as yet; but receive power as kings one hour with the beast.

These have one mind, and shall give their power and strength unto the beast. —REVELATION 17:9-13

The first kingdom was the Babylonian or Egyptian Empire; the second, the Assyrian; the third, the great Babylonian Empire under Nebuchadnezzar and his grandson, Belshazzar.

When Israel began to fall away from God, the first great Gentile empire to form was the Assyrian. The Babylonians then overthrew the Assyrian Empire by dissolving it into their own. At the time of the Babylonian

Empire, Daniel delivers his prophecies concerning the development of the Gentile empires.

The fourth head was the Medo-Persian Empire. Daniel 5:5-31 records the account of the handwriting that appeared on the wall. It told of the Babylonian Empire's destruction and the rise of the Medes and the Persians. This fourth empire gave way to the fifth, the Greek Empire under Alexander the Great. When it collapsed, the sixth, the Roman Empire, swallowed it up.

The sixth head (kingdom) in John's vision existed when John received his prophecy. It was in his day that Jesus came to earth the first time to lay the foundation of His Church as its Chief Cornerstone. Then the apostles began building on that foundation after His resurrection. The Church has been accomplishing an extremely productive work during its approximately two thousand years on earth that has spanned the time separating the sixth and seventh heads of the system. The coming of Jesus Christ struck Satan a tremendous mortal blow. The Beast System collapsed with the fall of the Roman Empire.

Examining these biblical/historical truths gives us good understanding of what God is doing. As long as the

Church is on the earth carrying out Jesus' ministry of demonstrating God's mercy, the system cannot return to full operation.

But we are presently watching the system being prefabricated. After the Church is caught up, the Antichrist will fit the pieces together. In his season he will resurrect the system that produced the sixth head that was wounded unto death, the Roman Empire.

The harlot will have gathered multitudes expecting a false messiah — and the Beast will fulfill their false hopes. She will even rule in harmony with the Beast for a season, with her many false gods.

But when the fullness of the harlot's season comes in the last day's of her appearing, Satan will demand the world's worship of only one false god. That god will be the devil himself, and he will destroy the harlot before God destroys every other satanic institution that has opposed God's will.

> *And the angel said unto me, Wherefore didst thou marvel? I will tell thee the mystery of the woman, and of the beast that carrieth her, which hath the seven heads and ten horns.*

The beast that thou sawest was, and is not; and shall ascend out of the bottomless pit, and go into perdition: and they that dwell on the earth shall wonder, whose names were not written in the book of life from the foundation of the world, when they behold the beast that was, and is not, and yet is.

And here is the mind which hath wisdom. The seven heads are seven mountains, on which the woman sitteth.

And there are seven kings: five are fallen, and one is, and the other is not yet come; and when he cometh, he must continue a short space.

And the beast that was, and is not, even he is the eighth, and is of the seven, and goeth into perdition.

And the ten horns which thou sawest are ten kings, which have received no kingdom as yet; but receive power as kings one hour with the beast.

These have one mind, and shall give their power and strength unto the beast.

These shall make war with the Lamb, and the Lamb shall overcome them: for he is Lord of

191

lords, and King of kings: and they that are with him are called, and chosen, and faithful.

And he saith unto me, The waters which thou sawest, where the whore sitteth, are peoples, and multitudes, and nations, and tongues.

And the ten horns which thou sawest upon the beast, these shall hate the whore, and shall make her desolate and naked, and shall eat her flesh, and burn her with fire.

For God hath put in their hearts to fulfil his will, and to agree, and give their kingdom unto the beast, until the words of God shall be fulfilled.

And the woman which thou sawest is that great city, which reigneth over the kings of the earth. —REVELATION 17:7-18

According to John, once the seventh head, or kingdom, over which the harlot will reign becomes operational under the Antichrist, it will only last for a short season (the first three-and-one-half years of the Tribulation). During this time, the Antichrist will bring together the governments, armies, commerce, and religions of his ten-nation confederacy. And he will use the harlot system to advance himself to the center of world religion.

The ten kings of the ten nations will enter into a strong agreement with the Antichrist, pledging him their armies and their influence.

THE DESTRUCTION OF THE HARLOT

But when the Antichrist is ready to pursue his ambition to become God, he will have to destroy the religious system in order to rule unopposed as the world's spiritual leader. So, hating the influence of the harlot upon their people, the Antichrist and the False Prophet will use the military power of the ten nations to quickly destroy her. The national leaders will happily accommodate, because the religious systems the harlot represents at the height of her season will have been a great irritation to them.

The harlot today is not any single denominational structure. She is an amalgamation of all the world's ecclesiastical, man-made religions, including the present-day denominations choosing to have only a form of godliness. And she is about to receive a new vehicle through which she can function. Quite possibly it is the World Council of Churches, which works for unity of all religions.

We know the city destroyed at mid-Tribulation will be the headquarters of the harlot religious system or, as some have identified it, the world church. But its exact identity is unknown. Presently it is Geneva, Switzerland, headquarters of the World Council of Churches, World Bank center and city of treaties between nations.

Instead of being sidetracked with the Beast's different facets, we need to view the system as a whole. Just remember: its major parts are presently being prefabricated and it will be an amazing man who brings together into one operation these pieces of governments, commerce, armies and the harlot religious system. Then when her own prophetic season comes into fruition, she will be harvested in accordance with God's will.

If you know anyone who is sliding in through the harlot's deceptively laced gates into hell, pray for them! Pray that the barbs on God's fence surrounding hell will prick their heart through the blood of Jesus, the Gospel, the Holy Spirit, and the name of Jesus. Pray that God will send a laborer across their path; someone who could represent the mercy of God as no one else could do. And always be open to the possibility that, that witness could be you!

CHAPTER 13

THE SEASON OF
JESUS' RETURN

CHAPTER THIRTEEN

THE SEASON OF JESUS' RETURN

So Christ was once offered to bear the sins of many; and unto them that look for him shall he appear the second time without sin unto salvation. —HEBREWS 9:28

When the Seasons of Christ's appearing and the Tribulation's fulfillments have been harvested in full, the ultimate prophetic fulfillment of the Church Age, the return of Jesus Christ, will finally come to pass.

When Jesus returns to earth, He will deal with sin, but not in the way He dealt with it the first time He came to earth. Jesus came the first time to bear the sins of many. The second time Jesus comes, however, He will destroy the followers of Satan, who rejected His sacrifice. His return will fulfill the Old Testament prophet's long heralded, "Day of the Lord."

THE DAY OF THE LORD
BATTLE OF ARMAGEDDON

Behold, the day of the LORD cometh [the day He returns to establish His Kingdom], *and thy spoil shall be divided in the midst of thee.*

For I will gather all nations against Jerusalem to battle [the Battle of Armegeddon]; *and the city shall be taken, and the houses rifled, and the women ravished; and half of the city shall go forth into captivity, and the residue of the people shall not be cut off from the city.*

Then shall the LORD go forth, and fight against those nations, as when he fought in the day of battle.

And his feet shall stand in that day upon the mount of Olives, which is before Jerusalem on the east, and the mount of Olives shall cleave in the midst thereof toward the east and toward the west, and there shall be a very great valley; and half of the mountain shall remove toward the north, and half of it toward the south.

And ye shall flee to the valley of the mountains; for the valley of the mountains shall reach unto

Azal: yea, ye shall flee, like as ye fled from before the earthquake in the days of Uzziah king of Judah: and the LORD my God shall come, and all the saints with thee. —ZECHARIAH 14:1-5

In this revealing passage of Zechariah we are given a glimpse of the exact day on which Jesus Christ will return. Other Old Testament prophets spoke of its coming and the judgments that awaited those to whom Christ would come. But Zechariah gives us a detailed scenario of various activities that will happen on the day itself.

Verse 5 reveals Jesus' actual return, including those who will return with him to the earth. Zechariah tells us that when the Lord returns from heaven to stand upon the Mount of Olives for the Battle of Armageddon, all the saints will return with Him. So the saints will have to be with Jesus in heaven to be able to return with Him to earth. This is a thrilling and exciting revelation of Christ's Second Coming which harmonizes with the seventh angelic trumpet of Revelation 11.

CHANGES IN LIGHT

Now in Zechariah 14:6 the Battle of Armageddon begins:

And it shall come to pass in that day, that the light shall not be clear, nor dark.

When the season of Jesus Christ's second coming is ready to be harvested, for a brief period of time, there will be no natural light from the sun, moon, or stars. According to Revelation 16:10, natural light will be withheld from "the seat of the beast," meaning the geographical area over which the Antichrist will have gained control. Some think he will control the whole world, but he never does. He would like to, but God interferes.

On this last day of the Tribulation — the day Jesus is to return — there will be some light, but it will not increase. The sky will remain a sort of eerie gray.

But it shall be one day which shall be known to the Lord, not day, nor night: but it shall come to pass, that at evening time it shall be light (v. 7).

Why would it be light at a time when it would ordinarily be getting dark? Because the Battle of Armageddon will be over by then. By that point of this coming season, those who have been destroying the earth will have been destroyed. The Antichrist and False Prophet will have been thrown into the lake of fire. Satan will have been bound and cast into prison[1] for a thousand years. Jesus will have taken over the governments of the world and as He begins His thousand-year reign. It will be so glorious that at evening the sun will be bright!

> *And it shall be in that day, that living waters shall go out from Jerusalem; half of them toward the former sea, and half of them toward the hinder sea: in summer and in winter shall it be* (v.8).

A great earthquake[2] alluded to in verse 4 will divide the Mount of Olives to make a port out of the city of Jerusalem. Waters will flow from one sea to the other — the Mediterranean to the Dead Sea.

> *And the LORD shall be king over all the earth: in that day shall there be one LORD, and his name one.*

> *All the land shall be turned as a plain from Geba to Rimmon south of Jerusalem: and it shall be lifted up, and inhabited in her place, from Benjamin's gate unto the place of the first gate, unto the corner gate, and from the tower of Hananeel unto the king's winepresses.*

---

[1] The Bottomless Pit. (See Revelation 20:1-3.)

[2] This is the earthquake prophesied by Jesus in Revelation 6:12.

And men shall dwell in it, and there shall be no more utter destruction; but Jerusalem shall be safely inhabited.

And this shall be the plague wherewith the LORD will smite all the people that have fought against Jerusalem (vvs.9-12).

All the armies[3] Satan will be able to gather to come against Jerusalem for the Battle of Armageddon will be gathered in the valley of Megiddo, stretching into the plains of Jezreel. The Lord will stand on the Mount of Olives. Then He will speak the Word as it goes forth out of His mouth like a two-edged sword to destroy the armies of the Antichrist:

Their flesh shall consume away while they stand upon their feet, and their eyes shall consume away in their holes, and their tongues shall consume away in their mouth.

And it shall come to pass in that day, that a great tumult from the LORD shall be among them;

---

[3] The Antichrist will bring ten armies to the Battle of Armageddon (see Rev. 17:10-14.) He will also have the support of the Orientals of Revelation 9:13-19 and 16:12,16.

and they shall lay hold every one on the hand of his neighbour, and his hand shall rise up against the hand of his neighbour. And Judah also shall fight at Jerusalem; and the wealth of all the heathen round about shall be gathered together, gold, and silver, and apparel, in great abundance.

And so shall be the plague of the horse, of the mule, of the camel, and of the ass, and of all the beasts that shall be in these tents, as this plague (vvs. 12-15).

In this rapidly approaching season, Jesus will speak the Word from the Mount of Olives that will release a plague which smites the vast armies of the Antichrist (Zechariah 14:12). Then those gathered against him will be immediately blinded as their eyes are consumed away in their sockets. They will also be struck immediately dumb as their tongues are consumed away in their mouths. In fright, they will reach out and grab one another for security. But that will only frighten them more, and they will turn to fight among themselves. Their flesh will then fall away from their bones and their blood will gush to the earth, creating the immense pool of blood described in Revelation 14. It will cover an area of about 185 miles in the valley of Megiddo and the plains of Jezreel.

For those who remain hardened in their hearts throughout the Tribulation to oppose and face Jesus at this time in history, this season of His return will be their worst nightmare come true.

We have seen in Zechariah 14 that the events which will take place at the Lord's return to earth are distinctly different from those surrounding the Rapture. So you can readily see the distinct difference between Jesus Christ's return and His appearing.

To further distinguish the two events, let's look now at Revelation, chapters 19 and 20.

In Revelation 19:11, we pick up the final day of the Tribulation and the return of Christ to earth:

And I saw heaven opened, and behold a white horse; and he that sat upon him was called Faithful and True, and in righteousness he doth judge and make war.

(The rider in chapter 6 could not be personally identified because that rider was the Antichrist.) But we are able to identify the rider of this white horse. This rider is called Faithful and True. He is our Lord Jesus Christ! What does He do? **In righteousness he doth judge and make war.**

A GOD OF WRATH

Many people believe that our God has nothing to do with war. Others see Him as only a God of love, thinking they can live any way they choose and God will do nothing. Those people need to read the whole Book. Because there is more to the nature of God than just love. He is a God of anger, wrath, and furious indignation Who will not acquit the wicked. But of course He is also love, and has permitted us to meet Him in His love rather than in His wrath. When we discover the real love of God and all the aspects of His divine nature, we can understand His tremendous compassion for the lost, and wrathful disdain for sin.

John goes on with His description in Revelation 19:12,13,15:

His eyes were as a flame of fire, and on his head were many crowns; and he had a name written, that no man knew, but he himself.

And he was clothed with a vesture dipped in blood: and his name is called The Word of God.

And out of his mouth goeth a sharp sword, that with it he should smite the nations: and he shall rule them with a rod of iron; and he treadeth the winepress of the fierceness and wrath of Almighty God.

These closing verses of Revelation 19 are a preview of the Battle of Armageddon and the winepress that will create the vast pool of blood in the valley of Jezreel. (See Revelation 14:14-20.) Jesus is the one who will tread the winepress. Standing on the Mount of Olives, He will speak the Word of God that releases the plague of Zechariah 14:12 to destroy the armies gathered together against Him at the Battle of Armageddon.

And he hath on his vesture and on his thigh a name written, KING OF KINGS, AND LORD OF LORDS.

And I saw an angel standing in the sun; and he cried with a loud voice, saying to all the fowls that fly in the midst of heaven, Come and gather yourselves together unto the supper of the great God; That ye may eat the flesh of kings, and the flesh of captains, and the flesh of mighty men, and the flesh of horses, and of them that sit on them, and the flesh of all men, both free and bond, both small and great.

And I saw the beast, and the kings of the earth, and their armies, gathered together to make war against him that sat on the horse, and against his army.

And the beast, was taken, and with him the false prophet that wrought miracles before him, with which he deceived them that had received the mark of the beast, and them that worshipped his image. These both were cast alive into a lake of fire burning with brimstone.

And the remnant were slain with the sword of him that sat upon the horse, which sword proceeded out of his mouth: and all the fowls were filled with their flesh. —REVELATION 19:16-21

SATAN AND SIN DEFEATED!

Have you ever heard the phrase, "Read the back of the Book, because it says we win!"? Well here it is! Here is God's prophetic record of Jesus Christ and His Church's promised victory over the power of Satan and his evil rulers on this earth! The harvest of this coming season will be the enemies of Christ's destruction, that will usher in the Millennium, revealed in Revelation 20:

And I saw an angel come down from heaven, having the key of the bottomless pit and a great chain in his hand.

And he laid hold on the dragon, that old serpent, which is the Devil, and Satan, and bound him a thousand years,

And cast him into the bottomless pit, and shut him up, and set a seal upon him, that he should deceive the nations no more, till the thousand years should be fulfilled: and after that he must be loosed a little season.

And I saw thrones, and they sat upon them, and judgment was given unto them: and I saw the souls of them that were beheaded for the witness of Jesus, and for the word of God, and which had not worshipped the beast, neither his image, neither had received his mark upon their foreheads, or in their hands; and they lived and reigned with Christ a thousand years. —REVELATION 20:1-4

So in the season of Jesus' return, the Antichrist and his followers will be destroyed by the Word of Jesus' mouth. Satan will be chained and cast into prison for a thousand years. Then all the martyred saints of the

Tribulation Period will be resurrected to enter relationship with the Lord Jesus Christ and all the other saints.

These coming events will be distinctly different from those that will occur at the appearing of Christ to rapture His Church. But they will all work together to fulfill God's redemptive plan. The Church, that is ready at a moment's notice, will be caught up before the first day of the Tribulation Period. Then once the Great Tribulation has run its course, Jesus will return to establish His Kingdom, visibly on earth. In that season of eternal splendor, you and I will serve the Lord in resurrection bodies on a new and higher level of sharing His mercy with the world. Amen! This is exciting!

So look for Jesus everyday. Be among those who are watching, praying, and looking for His appearing in this the season of His appearing.

As you pray, ask for new opportunities to show God's mercy.

Then be alert to the people He sends across your path. It's harvest season and the day of Jesus Christ's appearing is nearer than ever! The fig tree and all the other trees are fully in bloom, and the fields are white!

CHAPTER 14

THE SEASON OF
THE MILLENNIUM

THE SEASON OF THE MILLENNIUM

And I saw an angel come down from heaven, having the key of the bottomless pit and a great chain in his hand.

And he laid hold on the dragon, that old serpent, which is the Devil, and Satan, and bound him a thousand years,

And cast him into the bottomless pit, and shut him up, and set a seal upon him, that he should deceive the nations no more, till the thousand years should be fulfilled: and after that he must be loosed a little season. —REVELATION 20:1-3

Following the judgmental destruction of God's enemies at the Battle of Armageddon, an amazing new season of redemption will begin. The saints of God will reign with Christ for a thousand years on earth.

Revelation 20:4 describes many occupied thrones!

And I saw thrones, and they sat upon them, and judgment was given unto them.... (v. 4).

The members of the Church in this coming season will receive their assignments for future duties while in heaven around God's throne and will return with Jesus to administrate His kingdom on earth.

During this coming season, a theocratic government will exist that will be a perfect administration. There will be no political parties, labor unions or police. Every position of authority, from the local level to the highest government official, will be filled by the saints who have returned with Jesus. In this season of Jesus' world rule, you or someone you know may be king of the United States!

AN ERA OF HEALTH AND PEACE

Satan's imprisonment will veritably negate his earthly operation. Since he is the only cause of death, sickness and temptation, these will become almost nonexistent. Longevity of life will be restored to the Millennium's natural people, who will continue to reproduce children.

There shall be no more thence an infant of days, nor an old man that hath not filled his days: for the child shall die an hundred years old; but the sinner being an hundred years old shall be accursed. —Isaiah 65:20

If one were to die at a hundred years old during the Millennium, he or she would still be considered a child. Any death during this coming thousand year season will result from sin in the hearts of unrighteous people who were not slain at the Battle of Armageddon who fail to repent.

Peace will extend to all animals.

The wolf also shall dwell with the lamb, and the leopard shall lie down with the kid; and the calf and the young lion and the fatling together; and a little child shall lead them. —Isaiah 11:6

Any creatures turned natural enemies by Adam's fall will be reconciled. Parents won't worry about their children. Even if a child should reach into the hole of a serpent, he will not be bitten.

...and I saw the souls of them that were beheaded for the witness of Jesus, and for the

word of God, and which had not worshipped the beast, neither his image, neither had received his mark upon their foreheads, or in their hands; and they lived and reigned with Christ a thousand years. —REVELATION 20:4

This verse in John's revelation describes the martyred saints of the Tribulation who were discovered when the fifth seal was opened. Resurrected on the first day of the Millennium, they will take their place with the Lord's victorious company, fully avenged.

THE RESURRECTION OF THE WICKED DEAD

At the end of the Millennium, the wicked dead from the time of Adam will be resurrected to be judged by God at the Great White Throne Judgment.

But during the Millennium, God will continue to reach out with His fourth phase of mercy to the survivors of the Tribulation who did not bow to the Antichrist. Rather than destroying them, God will offer them salvation.[1] They will live in peace and righteousness and

---

[1] The nations of Revelation 21:24-26 are saved during the Millennium. We know this because no unrighteousness can carry over onto the new earth.

multiply upon the earth. God will give all men every opportunity to receive Jesus during this fourth phase of His mercy, waiting until after the Millennium to judge the wicked.

THE FIRST RESURRECTION

But the rest of the dead lived not again until the thousand years were finished. This is the first resurrection.

Blessed and holy is he that hath part in the first resurrection: on such the second death hath no power, but they shall be priests of God and of Christ, and shall reign with him a thousand years. —REVELATION 20:5-6

The first resurrection includes all the raptures, or translations (four), and all resurrections (three), except the resurrection of the wicked dead.

Before the Tribulation begins, the Church is caught up. This involves the resurrection of the dead in Christ and the catching up of the living Christians. These two acts will form one major event. (1 Thessalonians. 4:16-18.)

Next, at mid-Tribulation, a great multitude, the converts of the 144,000, will be caught away to remove them from the path of the Antichrist's wrath. (Revelation 7:9-17.) When their ministry is completed some months later, the 144,000 Jewish evangelists will be taken up. (Revelation 14:1-5.)

On the final day of the Tribulation (also the first day of the Millennium), the Two Witnesses will be resurrected and taken up. (Revelation 11:3-12.) Then later that day, the martyred Tribulation saints will be resurrected. (Revelation 20:4.) The first resurrection will therefore be comprised of these seven distinct events.

SATAN IS RELEASED

Now when the thousand years have expired:

...Satan shall be loosed out of his prison,

And shall go out to deceive the nations which are in the four quarters of the earth, Gog and Magog, to gather them together to battle: the number of whom is as the sand of the sea.

And they went up on the breadth of the earth, and compassed the camp of the saints about, and the beloved city: and fire came down from God out of heaven, and devoured them.

*And the devil that deceived them was cast
into the lake of fire and brimstone, where the
beast and the false prophet are, and shall be
tormented day and night for ever and ever.* —
REVELATION 20:7-10

The four horsemen of the Apocalypse released by
seals one through four in John's Revelation destroy one-
fourth of the earth's population, the 200 million-man
Oriental army destroys another third, and the plagues
also take a toll. You can learn about all of this in great
detail in my book, Revelation Revealed. In it, you will find
verse by verse commentary on all of Revelation's events.

At the Tribulation's end, approximately[2] 35 to 40
percent of the earth's population will still be alive. These
will be people over whom Jesus has started to reign.
They will have to be cared for, ministered to, and put
back into a productive society. So Jesus will rule them
with a rod of iron (Rev. 19:15), or firm authority.

As I pointed out in chapter 12, many nations will be
saved during the Millennium. (Revelation 21:24.) But
even those who aren't saved will have to worship Jesus
during this season. (Zechariah 14:16,17.) Every person

---

[2] This is an educated guess. The number could actually be less.

who doesn't receive Jesus as Savior and Lord will have an opportunity to follow Satan when he is released from the bottomless pit at the end of the thousand year period. This is simply amazing. That sin will still carry the power to resist and reject even God's fourth powerful phase of mercy during Christ's physical, visible kingdom, is beyond reason. But it will happen, because sin is an evil that transcends reason.

Once Satan is released, he will go about the earth in one last desperate season to deceive as many nations as possible. When God restores the power of choice by allowing both good and evil upon the earth, Satan will gather a large following of people to lead them against the camp of the saints and the Holy City.

But God will send fire from heaven to end this strange battle, moving so swiftly that it will be as though the battle never actually occurred. Satan will again be taken captive, then cast into the lake of fire where the Antichrist and False Prophet will have been at that juncture for one thousand years. The only people left alive on the earth at that time will be the saints from all time periods, the righteous remnant of Israel, and the nations saved during Christ's reign.

Now, it is an intelligent question to ask, "why?" Satan will be released from the bottomless pit.

The answer is, our God is a just God. He will release Satan for a short span of time (perhaps for only a few weeks) to tempt the people who have lived during the physical reign of our Lord Jesus during the Millennium.

Understand that from the time of Adam everyone has been tempted by Satan and given the opportunity to overcome him. So, if Satan were not released at the end of the Millennium to tempt those who live through it (not the righteous Church), every other generation who had previously yielded to Satan and were lost could accuse God of being unjust.

THE GREAT WHITE THRONE JUDGMENT

In Revelation 20:11 the scene changes from earth to the throne room in heaven.

And I saw a great white throne, and him that sat on it, from whose face the earth and the heaven fled away; and there was found no place for them.

And I saw the dead, small and great, stand before God; and the books were opened: and another book was opened, which is the book of life: and the dead were judged out of those things which were written in the books, according to their works.

And the sea gave up the dead which were in it; and death and hell delivered up the dead which were in them: and they were judged every man according to their works.

And death and hell were cast into the lake of fire. This is the second death.

And whosoever was not found written in the book of life was cast into the lake of fire. — REVELATION 20:11-15

In this final resurrection at the end of the Millennium, the wicked dead of all ages will be resurrected to stand before God's throne. No one will be left on earth, and hell will be emptied.

While this judgment is taking place in heaven, earth and the heavens surrounding it will be destroyed. And God, as Judge, will sit on one side of His throne. He will be backed by angels and the righteous people of all ages: the Old and New Testament saints, the Tribulation saints, the nations saved during the Millennium and the godly angels.

First Corinthians 6:3 clearly states that the angels who did not keep their first estate will be judged by you and me, the Church. So waiting to be judged on the other side of God's throne will be all nations which did not turn to God before or after the Tribulation, and the fallen angels referred to in Jude 6: **And the angels which kept not their first estate, but left their own habitation, he hath reserved in everlasting chains under darkness unto the judgment of the great day.**

God will judge fallen mankind while His saints will judge fallen angels at the Great White Throne. God will judge the unrighteous according to their works recorded in the book He opens. Afterwards, He will assign them to their final place of punishment, the lake of fire. This is the second death, a state of eternal death! What little God's Word tells us about the lake of fire is enough to reveal that no person in his right mind would want to be part of it.

But the righteous will never see the second death. We will be ruling the world during the Millennium's righteous reign of Jesus Christ as His kings and priests. With vested authority, we will judge the world.

You don't want anyone you know to miss this thrilling fulfillment of redemptive history. So share, preach, teach, pray, and expect the Holy Spirit to confirm God's Word of truth through healings, wonders, and miraculous signs with everyone you know who isn't ready to rule. Because in the coming season of the Millennium, the saints will reign!

CHAPTER 15

THE FINAL SEASON —
ETERNITY

CHAPTER FIFTEEN

THE FINAL SEASON — ETERNITY

Following the Great White Throne Judgment prophesied by John in Revelation 20, God will be ready to bring about mankind's final season of divine redemption.

At the end of the Millennium, no people remain on earth. The wicked will be in the lake of fire, and the righteous will be in heaven awaiting God's next great act — the creation of a new heaven, new earth, and the New Jerusalem.

Peter describes the destruction of the earth and its immediate heavens which will take place during the final judgment:

> *But the day of the Lord will come as a thief in the night; in the which the heavens shall pass away with a great noise, and the elements shall melt with fervent heat, the earth also and the works that are therein shall be burned up.* —2 PETER 3:10

So God will create a new earth surrounded by a new heaven where His kingdom will continue forever in this final season of man's redemption.

Revelation 21 opens with John's description of this final season of redemptive history's new heaven, earth, and Jerusalem. Containing no large bodies of water, the new earth will be larger in land area than the former earth.

And I saw a new heaven and a new earth: for the first heaven and the first earth were passed away; and there was no more sea.

And I John saw the holy city, new Jerusalem, coming down from God out of heaven, prepared as a bride adorned for her husband. —REVELATION 21:1,2

And he shewed me a pure river of water of life, clear as crystal, proceeding out of the throne of God and of the Lamb.

In the midst of the street of it, and on either side of the river, was there the tree of life, which bare twelve manner of fruits, and yielded her fruit every month: and the leaves of the tree were for the healing of the nations.

And there shall be no more curse: but the throne of God and of the Lamb shall be in it; and his servants shall serve him:

And they shall see his face; and his name shall be in their foreheads.

And there shall be no night there; and they need no candle, neither light of the sun; for the Lord God giveth them light: and they shall reign for ever and ever.

And he said unto me, These sayings are faithful and true: and the Lord God of the holy prophets sent his angel to shew unto his servants the things which must shortly be done.

Behold, I come quickly: blessed is he that keepeth the sayings of the prophecy of this book.

And I John saw these things, and heard them. And when I had heard and seen, I fell down to worship before the feet of the angel which shewed me these things.

Then saith he unto me, See thou do it not: for I am thy fellowservant, and of thy brethren the prophets, and of them which keep the sayings of this book: worship God.

And he saith unto me, Seal not the sayings of the prophecy of this book: for the time is at hand.

He that is unjust, let him be unjust still: and he which is filthy, let him be filthy still: and he that is righteous, let him be righteous still: and he that is holy, let him be holy still.

And, behold, I come quickly; and my reward is with me, to give every man according as his work shall be.

I am Alpha and Omega, the beginning and the end, the first and the last.

Blessed are they that do his commandments, that they may have right to the tree of life, and may enter in through the gates into the city.

For without are dogs, and sorcerers, and whoremongers, and murderers, and idolaters, and whosoever loveth and maketh a lie.

I Jesus have sent mine angel to testify unto you these things in the churches. I am the root and the offspring of David, and the bright and morning star.

And the Spirit and the bride say, Come. And let him that heareth say, Come. And let him that is athirst come. And whosoever will, let him take the water of life freely.

For I testify unto every man that heareth the words of the prophecy of this book, If any man shall add unto these things, God shall add unto him the plagues that are written in this book:

And if any man shall take away from the words of the book of this prophecy, God shall take away his part out of the book of life, and out of the holy city, and from the things which are written in this book.

He which testifieth these things saith, Surely I come quickly. Amen. Even so, come, Lord Jesus.

The grace of our Lord Jesus Christ be with you all. Amen. —REVELATION 22:1-21

Only the righteous will live on the new earth. So you don't want to miss it! The New Jerusalem will be majestic — beautiful like a jasper stone! Clear as crystal! It will have a great high wall around it with an angel at each of its twelve gates. God's river of life will rush out from His throne through the city feeding His tree of life. Day and night will cease to exist. And we will again, see God's face!

THE NEW JERUSALEM

The wall of the New Jerusalem will have twelve foundations on which the names of the Lamb's twelve apostles will be written. It will be 1,500 miles square (not square miles), which will be equivalent of 2,250,000 square miles per level.[1] Los Angeles, the largest American city in land area, covers more than 500 square miles. But the New Jerusalem will be 1,500 miles north to south, east to west, and 1,500 miles high! If it were placed on the United States, it would fit laterally between the Rocky and Appalachian Mountains, longitudinally between the Canadian border and the Gulf of Mexico.

Some people have taught that so few of us will be in this vast city that we might not see another child of God for years.

But I say, they are wrong! We are going to have plenty of company, because Jesus said His Father's house will be filled. (See Luke 14:16-24.) The strands on God's fence that currently guard hell and the four phases of His mercy will ensure it to be so. What a blessed fellowship this will be! So, the Church has a great job to do in this hour!

---

[1] Nothing in Scripture gives insight as to how many levels there may be.

Oh, I'm telling you that you don't want to miss this coming eternal season in which we will walk and talk with God as Adam did before the garden fall. You don't want anyone you know to miss this coming season either. So be dilligent about your soulwinning call. Remember, as a soulwinner appointed by Jesus, all you really have to do is "look"...because the Lord has already guaranteed a boat-sinking catch. Simply remember to ask the Lord every day to send someone across your path. Then be sensitive to every situation that presents itself.

As this perfect eternal season approaches, my spirit rejoices in the excitement of its anticipation. We are currently in the Last Days Harvest of Souls that will lead up to the season of His appearing, that will lead to the season of the Tribulation, that will lead the season of Christ's second coming, that will lead to the Millennium, that will lead to the new heavens and new earth. Hallelujah!

Revelation 21:27 reveals all people who defile, work abominations, and lie will have already been cast into the lake of fire. They will have no part in the new heaven, new earth or New Jerusalem.

Combined together on the new earth in this eternal season will be:

- A righteous people in mortal bodies like Adam and Eve before the Fall.

- The natural seed of Abraham, the nation of Israel, who will be fully restored during the Millennium, in mortal bodies. (See Isaiah 35; Ezekiel 36:11.)

- The Church, the only inhabitants with glorified bodies, who live in New Jerusalem and continue serving as administrators of Jesus' everlasting kingdom.

GOD'S PLANS ARE ALWAYS PERFECT

Keep in mind that everything God has done was and is perfect. Though Satan hindered God's plan in the Garden of Eden, God's plan was no less perfect. He saw Adam and Eve's deception coming and immediately gave the first Gospel (The Proto Evangelum), announcing the crushing of the serpent's head (Genesis 3:15). Then He called Abraham, whose family brought forth Jesus Who brought forth His Church. (Galatians 3:14.) And today we are a mighty force to be reckoned with spiritually in the earth.

And Jesus came and spake unto them, saying, All power is given unto me in heaven and in earth. —MATTHEW 28:18

God hasn't changed His mind about having a perfect mortal being. Neither has He changed His mind about having a perfect nation of people such as Israel.

Go ye therefore, and teach all nations, baptizing them in the name of the Father, and of the Son, and of the Holy Ghost.... —MATTHEW 28:19

He is bringing His Church into perfection through the ministry of apostles, prophets, evangelists, pastors and teachers. (Ephesians 4:11-16.)

Teaching them to observe all things whatso-ever I have commanded you... —MATTHEW 28:20

The healing revivals have come and gone, and today we have come into our own. We have a knowledge of God's Word no generation before has ever had before us, and we believe in the miracle power of His Holy Spirit! Our message and our preaching need not come in mere words of wisdom, but in demonstration of the Spirit and power, so those we preach to will see God's demonstration as we minister His mercy in setting them free! (2 Corinthians 2:4,5.)

When man's season is complete, God will have brought every part of His plan together on the new earth.

As we overcome today in the Church in our present season, we will be rewarded with our glorified bodies — to be just like Jesus — the "last Adam" — in the next season. (1 Corinthians 15:54; Hebrews 12:2; 1 Corinthians 15:51-53; 1 John 3:1-3.) Then, finally, we will be like Adam was, before sin brought the Fall. What a beautiful scene that will be!

THE SEASON OF HIS APPEARING

So tell everyone about it. The season of His appearing is NOW IN SEASON. Get out in the fields. Get involved in God's Last Days Harvest. Never let a day go by in which you don't ask God to send someone your way with whom you may share the Gospel in power and deed. Stay in God's Word, and make a new commitment to prayer.

And every day be sure to look up. Look up for the Lord's encouragement. Look up for the Holy Spirit's guidance. Look up for His soon appearance, because IT WILL HAPPEN IN A MOMENT'S NOTICE. Your redemption is drawing near!

>...*and, lo, I am with you alway, even unto the end of the world. Amen.* —MATTHEW 28:20

ABOUT THE AUTHOR

Dr. Hilton Sutton is regarded by many people as the nation's foremost authority on Bible prophecy as related to world affairs and current events.

An ordained minister of the Gospel and author of several books, Dr. Sutton earned his Th.D. from Jerusalem Cornerstone University and Seminary and served as pastor for several years before entering his present prophetic assignment. Today he travels throughout the world, taking the words of the most accurate news report ever — the Word of God — as it relates to the news today into his prophecy seminars around the world.

Having spent over thirty years researching and studying the book of Revelation, Dr. Sutton explains Bible prophecy and world affairs in a way that is clear, concise and easy to understand. He presents his messages on a layman's level and shows the Bible to be the most accurate, up-to-date book ever written.

Hilton Sutton and his family make their home in Humble, Texas, where he serves as president of Mission to America, a Christian organization dedicated to carrying the Gospel of Jesus Christ to the world. He is also president of Hilton Sutton Ministries, and has served as president of World Ministry Fellowship, an interdenominational ministerial and church fellowship located in Dallas, Texas.

In addition, Dr. Sutton is the national president of the Christian Evangelical Zionist Congress of America and serves on the board of the National Christian Leadership Conference for Israel located in New York City. His weekly telecast, "The Ancient Prophecies," can be seen on various Christian television stations across the country.

To receive Hilton Sutton's
monthly publication, "Update,"
write:
Mission to America
Hilton Sutton Ministries
736 Wilson Road
Humble, Texas 77338

Please include your prayer requests
and comments when you write.

The Harrison House Vision

Proclaiming the truth and the power

Of the Gospel of Jesus Christ

With excellence;

Challenging Christians to

Live victoriously,

Grow spiritually,

Know God intimately.